OECD
ECONOMIC SURVEYS

UNITED STATES

ORGANISATION FOR ECONOMIC CO-OPERATION AND DEVELOPMENT

ORGANISATION FOR ECONOMIC CO-OPERATION AND DEVELOPMENT

Pursuant to Article 1 of the Convention signed in Paris on 14th December 1960, and which came into force on 30th September 1961, the Organisation for Economic Co-operation and Development (OECD) shall promote policies designed:

- to achieve the highest sustainable economic growth and employment and a rising standard of living in Member countries, while maintaining financial stability, and thus to contribute to the development of the world economy;
- to contribute to sound economic expansion in Member as well as non-member countries in the process of economic development; and
- to contribute to the expansion of world trade on a multilateral, non-discriminatory basis in accordance with international obligations.

The original Member countries of the OECD are Austria, Belgium, Canada, Denmark, France, Germany, Greece, Iceland, Ireland, Italy, Luxembourg, the Netherlands, Norway, Portugal, Spain, Sweden, Switzerland, Turkey, the United Kingdom and the United States. The following countries became Members subsequently through accession at the dates indicated hereafter: Japan (28th April 1964), Finland (28th January 1969), Australia (7th June 1971) and New Zealand (29th May 1973). The Commission of the European Communities takes part in the work of the OECD (Article 13 of the OECD Convention).

Publié également en français.

Table of contents

Boxes

Tables

Statistical and structural annex

Diagrams

Text

BASIC STATISTICS OF THE UNITED STATES

THE LAND

Area (1 000sq.km)	9 373	Population of major cities, including their metropolitan areas (1.4.1990 estimates):
		New York 18 087 000
		Los Angeles-Anaheim-Riverside 14 532 000
		Chicago-Gary-Lake Country 8 066 000

THE PEOPLE

Population, 1991	252 711 000	Civilian labour force, 1991	125 303 000
Number of inhabitants per sq.km	27.0	*of which:*	
Population, annual net natural increase (average 1978-89)	2 619 200	Employed in agriculture	3 233 000
		Unemployed	8 426 000
Annual net natural increase, per cent (1978-89)	1.02	Net civilian immigration (annual average 1985-88)	666 000

PRODUCTION

Gross domestic product in 1991 (billions of US$)	5 694.9	Origin of national income in 1991 (per cent of national income[1]):	
GDP per head in 1991 (US$)	22 535	Agriculture, forestry and fishing	2.0
Gross fixed capital formation:		Manufacturing	18.5
Per cent of GDP in 1991	11.8	Construction and mining	5.4
Per head in 1991 (US$)	2 652.9	Government and government enterprises	15.4
		Other	58.7

THE GOVERNMENT

Government purchases of goods and services, 1991 (per cent of GDP) 19.1

Revenue of federal, state and local governments, 1991 (per cent of GDP) 30.7

Federal government debt as per cent of receipts from the public, 1991 105.1

Composition of the 102nd Congress 1992:

	House of Representatives[2]	Senate
Democrats	266	57
Republicans	166	43
Independents	1	—
Vacancies	2	—
Total	435	100

FOREIGN TRADE

Exports:		Imports:	
Exports of goods and services as per cent of GDP in 1991	10.5	Imports of goods and services as per cent of GDP in 1991	10.9
Main exports, 1991 (per cent of merchandise exports):		Main imports, 1991 (per cent of merchandise imports):	
Machinery and transport equipment	46.7	Machinery and transport equipment	43.3
Food and live animals	7.4	Food and live animals	4.5
Crude materials (inedible)	6.4	Crude materials (inedible)	2.7
Chemicals	10.7	Chemicals	5.0
Manufactured goods	8.9	Manufactured goods	11.8
All other	19.9	All other	32.7

1. Without capital consumption adjustment.
2. As of September 15, 1992, New York and North Carolina each had one vacancy.
Note: An international comparison of certain basic statistics is given in an annex table.

This Survey is based on the Secretariat's study prepared for the annual review of the United States by the Economic and Development Review Committee on 17th September 1992.

•

After revisions in the light of discussions during the review, final approval of the Survey for publication was given by the Committee on 8th October 1992.

•

The previous Survey of the United States was issued in November 1991.

Introduction

When last year's *Survey* was published, the U.S. economy was about begun to come out of recession. Although the recovery has continued despite fears of a further relapse, activity has remained sluggish, and unemployment has continued to rise. Inflationary pressures have been abating, and the underlying current-account position has improved significantly. OECD projections are for the continuation of slow gains in activity and employment, accompanied by a further mild disinflation and some slight renewed widening of the external deficit. Chapter I of the present *Survey* first reviews the nature of the on-going recovery process, with particular attention to private-sector adjustment of indebtedness and the constraints on macroeconomic policy action. It goes on to assess the short-term outlook for the economy.

In many respects the 1980s was a decade of success for the U.S. economy. It was among the few that created new employment on a massive scale while inflation was brought down. But at the same time, private saving fell, public-sector deficits rose and debts to the rest of the world built up. This course could not be sustained indefinitely. The need for raising saving is now indisputable, in order to put the U.S. economy onto a more sustainable medium-term growth path, by allowing for stronger investment without intensified calls on foreign capital and consequent pressures on interest rates world-wide. Chapter II first documents medium-term trends in incomes, productivity, investment and saving and makes the case for higher U.S. saving. Chapter III then goes on to examine the chronic problem of the Federal budget deficit, one of the major drags on U.S. saving. It reviews past approaches that have failed to achieve the goal of deficit reduction and then discusses various more direct options to fulfil this objective.

Long-term growth can be higher only if new investment opportunities are created and seized as they arise. Structural reform helps to open up such opportunities and raise investment. The United States was a champion of deregulation moves in the 1970s and early 1980s, but the pace of reform has slowed in the last several years. Chapter IV follows up on banking reform, which was treated extensively in the previous *Survey,* and also discusses the state of trade policy. Chapter V is then devoted to the review of the health-care system. It analyses the problem of explosive spending growth and lack of insurance coverage for a large number of citizens, and it provides an evaluation of various reform options, drawing on the experience of other OECD countries. Overall conclusions are presented in a final chapter.

I. Recent developments, policies and prospects

A hesitant recovery

The first quarter of 1992 marked the fastest economic growth in three years, as GDP rose 2.9 per cent at an annual rate. Slow growth began in early 1989, following the tightening of monetary conditions by the Federal Reserve, aimed at reducing inflationary pressures. GDP fell for three quarters beginning in the third quarter of 1990 when Iraq invaded Kuwait, and the unemployment rate moved up a percentage point, to 6½ per cent. By the second quarter of 1991, the economy began to revive, as monetary policy had eased substantially starting in the fall of 1990, and optimism returned with the end of the Gulf war. But while output had stopped falling, growth averaged only 1.2 per cent in the last three quarters of 1991, and the unemployment rate rose further, reaching 7.8 per cent in June 1992.

The strength in activity after the Gulf war was marked by many of the usual early signs of economic recovery: along with renewed business and consumer confidence, the stock market surged, and consumer spending began to recover, starting early in 1991. Housing construction, one of the main channels of influence of monetary policy, also moved up. With inventories quite lean, sales gains led quickly to increased production. On the other hand, business fixed investment continued to be weak.

While output continued to grow, spending lost momentum around mid-year. Housing starts stalled, perhaps influenced by an upward drift in mortgage interest rates. Firms did not start hiring on any significant scale, consumer confidence eventually faded, and consumer spending was flat from July to December. Two factors weighing down the economy's take-off in 1991 were business-sector construction and government purchases. Non-residential construction fell 12 per cent in 1991. About half of that decline came in office buildings, where vacancy

11

Diagram 1. **AGGREGATE ECONOMIC INDICATORS**

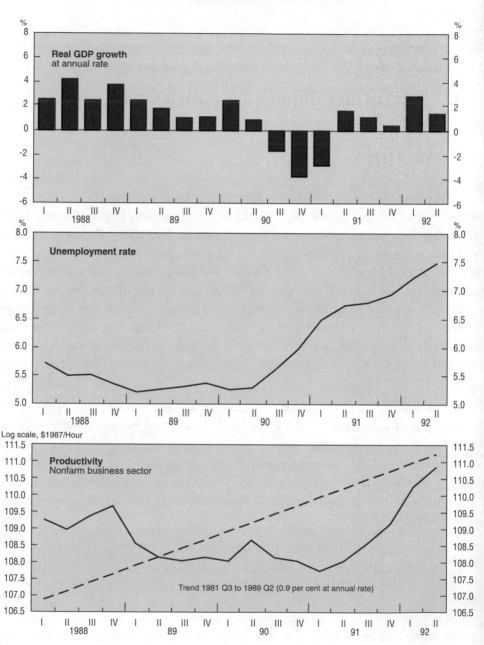

Source: Department of Labor, Bureau of Labor Statistics.

Diagram 2. **INVESTMENT TRENDS**

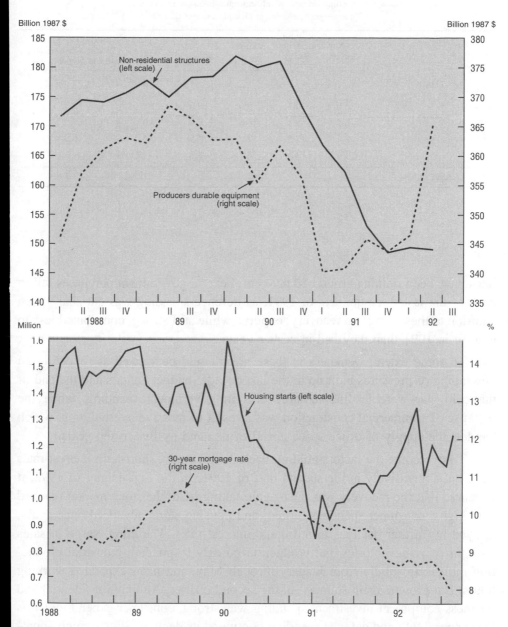

Sources: Department of Housing and Urban Development; Department of Commerce, Bureau of Economic Analysis and Census Bureau.

Table 1. **Investment intentions survey**

Plans for spending on new plant and equipment by business sector
Year-on-year percentage change, current dollars

	Oct-Nov. Survey	Jan-March Survey	Apr-May Survey	July-Aug Survey	Actual	*Memorandum item:* Business investment, national accounts basis
1988	7.3	8.8	10.7	10.6	11.0	9.6
1989	6.0	9.1	9.9	10.0	11.4	4.7
1990	6.7	8.1	6.8	5.4	5.0	1.2
1991	2.4	2.5	2.7	0.5	–0.6	–6.3
1992	5.4	4.6	4.7	4.3	–	–

Source: Census Bureau.

rates have been running around 20 per cent. Federal government purchases fell in each of the last three quarters of 1991, as defence spending was cut sharply. In addition to these drags on recovery, exports, while still strong, contributed less to growth in 1991 than they had in earlier years.

To some extent, weakness in these areas could be viewed as reflecting an unwinding of pressures built up in the last decade: budget deficits and the end of the cold war were leading to large cuts in government spending, while the collapse of commercial construction was a result of massive overbuilding, which has left the supply of office space ahead of demand by five to ten years.

To overcome the factors holding back the recovery, short-term interest rates were cut aggressively in the second half of 1991. In the first quarter of 1992, it appeared that the recovery was once again taking hold: the stock market reached new highs; consumer spending surged; and housing starts advanced once again, buoyed by further declines in mortgage interest rates. The initial surge in sales brought down inventories, but production quickly responded; industrial production moved up solidly from January through May, and firms expanded working hours. But growth again slumped in the second quarter. Although residential and business equipment investment spending was strong, consumer expenditure was flat, exports fell, and defence spending continued its decline. Slow growth apparently continued into the third quarter with stagnant private-sector employment, a

The change from GNP to GDP

In the November 1991 revision of the national accounts, the United States government changed its emphasis from Gross National Product (GNP) to Gross Domestic Product (GDP). GNP measures the production from the labour of, and capital owned by, residents of the United States and is therefore a good measure of the income of U.S. residents. GDP, on the other hand, measures production within the borders of the United States, and therefore emphasises production. The biggest difference between the two measures is net income from investments – that is, the difference between what U.S. residents earned on investments abroad and what foreign residents earned in the United States on their investments. In 1991, GNP exceeded GDP slightly – by $13.2 billion, or about 0.2 per cent – as U.S. residents earned more on their capital and labour abroad than foreign residents earned on their capital and labour in the United States.

GDP is more useful than GNP for analysing short-run economic activity in the United States since it is excludes income originating elsewhere. GDP is also a more accurate measure than GNP, since foreign investment earnings are difficult to measure. Also, the change puts the United States in step with other OECD countries, as twenty-two out of twenty-four Members now emphasise GDP rather than GNP.

downturn in exports and new orders for durables beginning in July and weakness in industrial production and construction spending as of August.

Labour productivity in the non-farm business sector has grown strongly recently and was up 2.5 per cent over the four quarters to the second quarter of 1992. While productivity growth typically picks up in the early stages of a recovery, the current situation is unusual, in that productivity has accelerated even though hours worked and employment have been flat or falling. There have been concerns that this boost in productivity may have restrained the recovery to the extent that employment prospects are an important factor in determining consumer sentiment. One factor behind the recent surge in productivity may have been its weakness when growth first began to slow in 1989. Then, productivity dropped sharply, as firms continued to hire after the initial fall-off in output growth. Because of this employment backlog, firms may subsequently have been able to expand output more than usual without needing to employ additional workers. As the scope for short-run labour-saving is used up and output continues to expand, firms will need to begin hiring.

Continuing improvement in external outcomes

1991 marked the fourth successive year of significant reduction in the U.S. external deficit. The merchandise-trade deficit dropped by $35 billion to $73 billion (1.3 per cent of GDP), and the current-account deficit, which had been as high as 3½ per cent of GDP in 1987, was virtually eliminated. Much of the improvement in the current account, though, was the result of one-time transfers of $43 billion associated with the Gulf War. Import volumes stagnated. Weakness was fairly widespread, as total domestic demand fell 1.8 per cent. Merchandise export volumes expanded by 6½ per cent in 1991, led by non-automotive capital goods and industrial supplies and materials. Exports were especially strong to Latin America representing about one-quarter of overall U.S. export growth in 1990 and 1991. Overall, market growth for manufactures remained near 5 per cent, and further gains of market shares were recorded. The surplus on non-factor services also widened by a further $13 billion in 1991, as exports increased 10 per cent while imports were up only 1½ per cent. Travel was among the most important contributors, with an increase in receipts of over 12 per cent.

The principal factor in strengthening trade outcomes is enhanced cost competitiveness. A variety of indicators point to continuing improvements due to labour-cost moderation and, most particularly, a renewed decline of the dollar.

Table 2. **Current account**

$ billion, seasonally adjusted annual rates

	1989	1990	1991	1991				1992	
				Q 1	Q 2	Q 3	Q 4	Q 1	Q 2
Current account balance	−106	−90	−4	49	10	−44	−29	−24	−71
Exports of goods, services and income	603	681	705	697	700	703	720	725	720
Imports of goods, services and income	698	738	717	705	706	724	731	720	761
Balances									
Goods	−116	−109	−73	−73	−66	−81	−74	−69	−98
Non-factor services	20	32	45	37	43	48	53	55	52
Investment income	−1	19	16	28	16	12	10	18	6
Private transfers	−1	−12	−13	−13	−13	−13	−13	−14	−14
Official transfers	−13	−21	21	70	30	−11	−4	−14	−17

Source: Department of Commerce, *Survey of Current Business.*

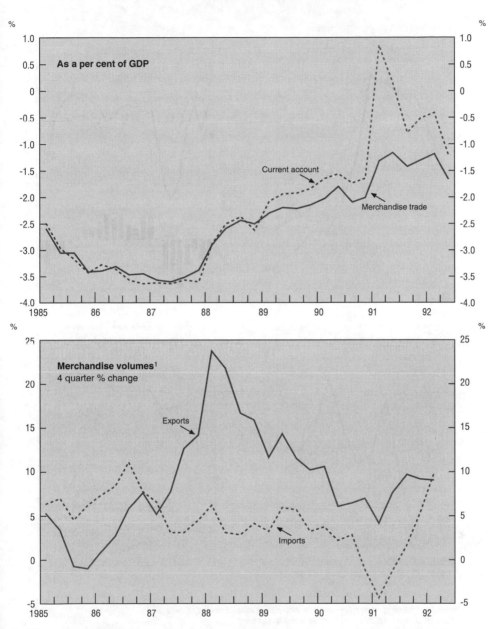

Diagram 3. **THE NARROWING EXTERNAL DEFICIT**

As a per cent of GDP

Current account

Merchandise trade

Merchandise volumes[1]
4 quarter % change

Exports

Imports

1. Balance of payments basis.
Source: U.S. Department of Commerce, Bureau of Economic Analysis.

Diagram 4. **FACTORS IN EXTERNAL TRADE PERFORMANCE**

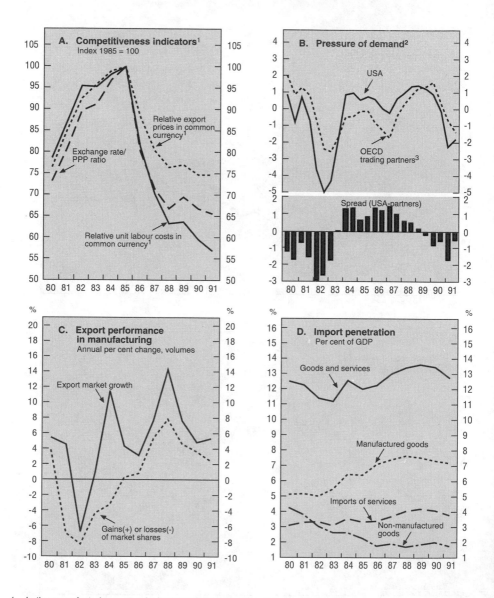

A. **Competitiveness indicators[1]**
Index 1985 = 100

Relative export prices in common currency[1]

Exchange rate/ PPP ratio

Relative unit labour costs in common currency[1]

B. **Pressure of demand[2]**

USA

OECD trading partners[3]

Spread (USA-partners)

C. **Export performance in manufacturing**
Annual per cent change, volumes

Export market growth

Gains(+) or losses(-) of market shares

D. **Import penetration**
Per cent of GDP

Goods and services

Manufactured goods

Imports of services

Non-manufactured goods

1. In the manufacturing sector. An increase indicates a loss of competitiveness.
2. Deviations of real total demand from its trend in per cent.
3. Aggregated using trade weights.
Source: OECD.

However, since 1988, there has been a slowdown in export market-share gains in line with the easing in the rate of depreciation and the weakening cyclical position of trading partners.

Net investment income fell slightly in 1991, as both gross receipts and payments shrunk owing to falling interest rates, slowing activity and declining profits in the United States and abroad. The balance on goods and services (including investment income) was in surplus in the first quarter of 1992 for the first time in a decade. The evolution of net unilateral transfers was most heavily influenced by the waning cash contributions from coalition partners during the Gulf War.

There are indications, however, that the underlying trend improvement in external outcomes may be stalling. The deficit on merchandise trade has fluctuated around $70 billion (at an annual rate) for the past six quarters, and the rise in the services surplus has moderated. Furthermore, the surplus on investment income in the second quarter of 1992 fell to its lowest level in over twenty years. Given the trend deterioration of net transfers and the cyclical recovery in the United States relative to its major trading partners, the external accounts may have already reached their low point for the cycle, even abstracting from the disappearance of the temporary effects of Gulf War contributions.

A similar conclusion is suggested by an analysis of saving and investment. While gross private saving rose 5.5 per cent in 1991 and is on track for an even greater rise this year, the recent surge in the Federal-government deficit on a national-accounts basis (from $166 billion in 1990 to $210 billion in 1991 and $294 billion at annual rates during the first half of 1992) and the improbability of a reversal any time soon points to little if any increase in gross domestic saving. However, gross domestic investment, which fell by nearly 10 per cent in 1991, looks set to rise cyclically.

Progress on inflation

Inflation has remained modest in the U.S. in 1992. In the twelve months to August, the overall consumer price index (CPI) rose 3.1 per cent, half the pace of 1990. At this rate, 1992 inflation would be the second lowest in 25 years; only in 1986 was it lower, and in that year, energy prices fell nearly 20 per cent. Softness

19

Diagram 5. **INFLATION IS COMING DOWN**

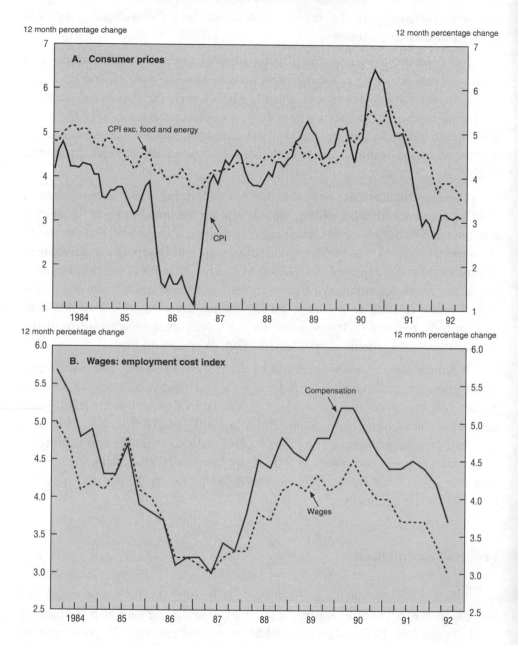

in food prices and some further declines in energy prices have helped moderate inflation in 1992, as was the case last year. Nonetheless, consumer prices excluding food and energy have also decelerated and were up only 3½ per cent in the latest twelve-month period, the best pace in 20 years.

Wage increases have also come down. Total hourly compensation of private-industry workers, as measured by the employment cost index (ECI), rose just 3¾ per cent over the twelve months to June 1992, down from 4½ per cent in 1990 and 4¾ per cent in 1988 and 1989. Wages and salaries decelerated even more, with an increase of just 3 per cent over the most recent twelve months, about as low as in 1986 and 1987. The cost of employee benefits continues to rise much faster than wages, at about a 5½ per cent pace, driven by increases in health-insurance costs. The on-going escalation of health-care costs is discussed in more detail in Chapter V.

Rough calculations of the natural rate of unemployment and the "sacrifice ratio" (the excess amount of unemployment needed for one year in order to reduce inflation by one percentage point) can be made from recent movements in inflation and the unemployment rate. Between 1987 and 1990, inflation picked up while unemployment averaged 5.4 per cent (1988 to 1990). Since 1990, inflation has fallen, while unemployment has averaged 6.9 per cent (1991 and 1992 first half). This suggests, as a rough calculation, that the natural rate of unemployment is between 5.4 and 6.9 per cent. The calculations included in Annex I suggest that the range can be narrowed to between 5½ to 6 per cent, although the range of uncertainty around these estimates is quite large. A related (and also rough) calculation can be made of the sacrifice ratio; it suggests that a ratio of between one-and-a-half and two is consistent with the recent evolution of inflation. Both of these results are close to consensus views before the recent slowdown began, suggesting that the disinflation seen so far has been about in line with historical experience.

Fiscal policy

The Federal government budget deficit rose substantially in 1991 and looks set to increase even further in 1992. On a consolidated basis – the broadest and most widely cited measure – the 1991 deficit was $269 billion, or 4¾ per cent of GDP, while the 1992 deficit is likely to be in the range of $330 billion, or about

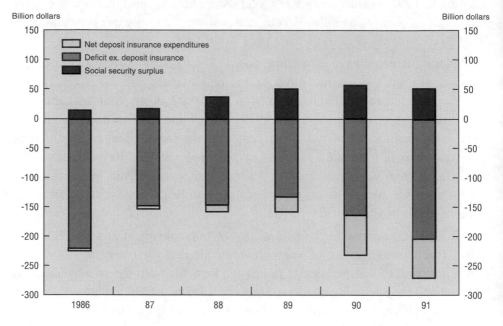

Diagram 6. **FEDERAL DEFICITS, CONSOLIDATED BASIS**
(fiscal years)

Source: Office of Management and Budget.

Table 3. **Budget deficit projections**
$ billion

	Fiscal years			
	1990	1991	1992	1993
Total deficit [1]	220	269	330	370
"On-budget" deficit (excluding social security)	277	321	380	427
Social security surplus [2]	57	52	50	57
National accounts deficit [3]	153	194	284	299
Deposit insurance expenditures	58	66	13	49
Memorandum				
National accounts deficit, calendar-year basis	166	210	309	296

1. Includes social security surplus and expenditures on deposit insurance.
2. Includes the (generally small) Postal Service net surplus.
3. Differs from the total deficit primarily by the exclusion of financial transactions, including those concerning deposit insurance.
Source: Congressional Budget Office; OECD estimates.

5¹/₂ per cent of GDP. This deterioration occurred despite the discipline of the 1990 Budget Enforcement Act (BEA), which, at the time it was enacted, was projected to lead to a balanced budget by 1995. Now, both the Congressional Budget Office (CBO) and the Office of Management and Budget (OMB) foresee deficits of more than $200 billion in that year.

The deteriorating budget situation over the last two years is partly the result of the recession and the ongoing resolution of the savings and loan debacle, both of which are allowed to change the deficit without triggering sanctions under the BEA. Still, according to CBO estimates, even allowing for these factors, the Federal deficit deteriorated by 0.3 per cent of GDP in 1991 and is likely to worsen by even more in 1992. The main source of this slippage is increased spending under existing programmes, mostly for health care, and an overestimate of tax receipts, especially from the capital-gains tax (as falling real-estate prices have led to a decline in such receipts). Such changes in "technical assumptions" are allowed to occur under the BEA, which prevents changes in laws that would boost the deficit but does nothing to constrain spending under existing laws that, for example, set criteria for eligibility but leave spending open-ended. The Budget Enforcement Act is discussed in more detail in Chapter III.

While the Budget Enforcement Act has made a useful contribution to containing the deficit – it most likely would have been larger without the Act – it is nonetheless inadequate to the task of eliminating the deficit. Institutional changes to control growth in mandatory-spending programmes (the "pay-as-you-go" provision) have been helpful, but the key contribution of the BEA stems from the tax increases and programme changes that were made "up front", at the time of enactment. The large spending cuts which have occurred in defence, which were incorporated as part of the BEA's goals, have also made an important contribution. As this experience suggests, there is no substitute for actually making the decisions on taxes and spending that will cut the deficit; proposals that promise a balanced budget without specifics will not work. This applies as much to proposals for balanced budget amendments to the Constitution as to legislative approaches. Specific proposals on the substantial further action on taxes and spending needed to put Federal finances on a sound basis are discussed in more detail in Chapter III.

Given the need to control the Federal budget deficit, there has been little scope for using fiscal policy to support demand in the economy. The

Administration's 1993 Budget proposed a small package of fiscal stimulus, including an investment tax credit, tax incentives for house-buying and a renewed appeal for capital-gains-tax relief. A package was passed by Congress, but it had been so modified that it was vetoed. A further package is before Congress at the time of writing. One element of stimulus was enacted by the President directly: he ordered a change in tax withholding schedules in order to reduce overpayment of taxes in 1992, which had the effect of immediately boosting take-home pay. The main cost to the government will be the lost interest on the overpaid taxes until they would have otherwise been refunded in mid-1993.

While it would be unwise to stimulate the economy with fiscal policy, given the size of the deficit and burgeoning public debt, some form of fiscal stimulus has been introduced during most downturns over the last half-century. According to CBO estimates, such stimulus has typically added about ¾ percentage point directly to growth in the early stages of recoveries. OECD calculations show that budgetary policy was rather less expansionary in 1991 than this, implying a limited drag on growth. Of course, the effects of fiscal policy cannot be viewed in a vacuum; it will be argued below that monetary policy as measured by the real Federal funds rate has been no more stimulative than has normally been the case.

It has been suggested that one area where the Treasury could take a more active role is in debt management. Current Treasury policy is to issue a roughly constant proportion of long- and short-term securities regardless of credit-market conditions. But as noted earlier, the spread between short- and long-term interest rates is currently at record levels – over 4 percentage points, suggesting that considerable sums could be saved by issuing more short-term securities, provided inflation and short-term interest rates remain low in the future. Moving toward shorter-maturity securities would also be a vote of confidence in the anti-inflationary stance of the Federal Reserve, since it would amount to a bet that interest rates would not rise as much as market participants anticipated – as would be the case if inflation came down more sharply than is implicit in market expectations. Such a vote of confidence might have the effect of lowering long-term interest rates. However, the evidence suggests that debt management has little impact on the yield curve in the United States, and theoretical arguments based on market efficiency make the same prediction. Also, a move to short-term securities raises transactions costs, since these securities must be "rolled over" more frequently.

State and local governments continued to run overall surpluses (including pension funds) in 1991, although these declined slightly from 1990 levels, largely on account of the weak economy. These surpluses had already shrunk substantially from mid-1980s levels, however, as many states began to run deficits on their current budgets. Since most states have a "balanced budget" requirement in one form or another, their weak financial situation led to a variety of spending cuts and tax increases which came into effect in 1991. (In many states, the statutory requirement for budget balance is quite weak, with the governor required only to submit for consideration a balanced budget, and no formal requirement for the legislatures to pass one. Also, surpluses from earlier years can often be drawn on in poor years.) States' balanced-budget policies put an obvious drag on spending in a weak economy, but this is not unusual, since such requirements have been in place for a long time. However, over the past decade, the Federal government has devolved responsibility for financing a number of public activities to states and localities, and its ongoing budgetary problems suggest continued pressure in this direction.

Debt developments

In the 1980s, debt grew much more rapidly than did nominal incomes. In recent years, debt growth has slowed considerably and lending in some categories, including bank loans and credit-card debt, has actually fallen. While the slowdown in debt growth is probably healthy on balance – some of the loans made during the boom in credit seem to have been made with unreasonable expectations – there has been concern that excessive caution on the part of borrowers and lenders may be significantly impeding the economic recovery. This is particularly true for the non-corporate business sector, which, in contrast to corporations and households, has not been able to benefit from the move toward increased securitisation of credit.

Lenders typically become more cautious when activity weakens: short-term growth prospects dim and lending becomes riskier. Banks respond by tightening lending standards, so that loans are denied to some businesses that earlier would have received them. As well, spreads between borrowing and lending widen to compensate for the additional risk. The 1990-91 recession was characterised by many of the usual signs of credit restraint: the Federal Reserve's Senior Loan

Diagram 7. RECENT CREDIT INDICATORS

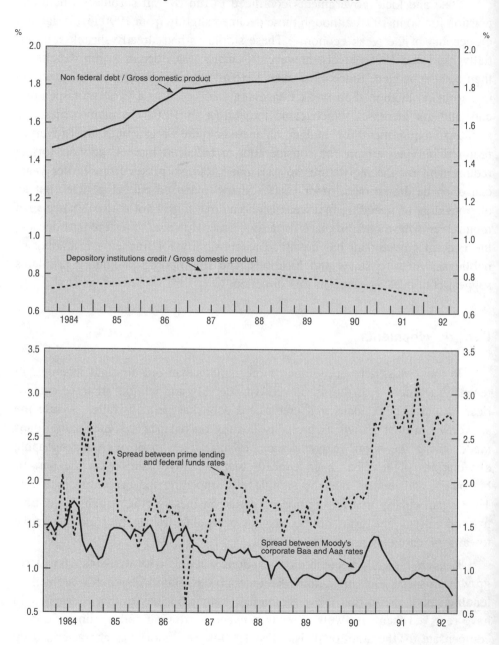

Source: Department of Commerce, *Survey of Current Business,* and Federal Reserve Board, *Flow of Funds Accounts.*

Officer Survey indicated a tightening of lending standards during 1990, for example, while banks cut lending rates by less than the fall in their cost of funds, and risk spreads between safer and lower-grade corporate bonds increased. As measured by the Senior Loan Officer Survey or the increase in corporate bond spreads, the severity of credit restrictions was about typical in the 1990-91 recession. One factor that may have made banks less willing to lend than usual has been the sharper focus on capital standards in recent years, beginning with the international standards agreed on at Basle in 1988 and reinforced by the emphasis of the 1991 Federal Deposit Insurance Corporation Improvement Act on capital (see Chapter IV for more details). The spread between bank's prime lending rate and cost of funds has been particularly wide, suggesting that the desire to boost capital may have had some impact.[2] Still, caution by lenders – a "credit crunch" – was probably not the most important factor in the 1990-91 recession.

By some measures, the degree of credit supply problems seems to have eased over the course of 1991 and into early 1992. By mid-1991, the Senior Loan Officer Survey was reporting that 80 to 90 per cent of banks were either leaving lending standards unchanged or, less frequently, easing them; by mid-1992, this was up to nearly 100 per cent. This is more favourable to expanded lending than it appears, since loan officers almost never report a reduction in lending standards, so that the lack of a tightening probably signals a loosening. Also, spreads

Table 4. **Senior loan officer survey**

Percentage of banks reporting tighter standards for approving business loan applications[1]

Three months ending with survey date	1990			1991				1992	
	May	Aug.	Oct.	Jan.	May	Aug.	Oct.	May	Aug.
Domestic bank lending to the following:									
Large firms	..	36	50	35	15	10	5	5	2
Middle market	58	43	48	37	16	14	13	4	2
Small businesses	54	34	41	32	9	9	7	0	0
Lending by U.S. branches and agencies of foreign banks	..	61[2]	72	89	28	0	11	11	11

1. Survey of sixty large domestically-chartered banks and eighteen U.S. branches and agencies of foreign banks.
2. Refers to tightening in the six-month period from February to August.
Source: Federal Reserve Board.

on risky securities had moved back to their pre-recession levels by mid-1991. However, banks' lending rates remain very high relative to their cost of funds, suggesting that "rationing by price" remains important in the banking sector.

For households, any reticence on the part of banks to lend would probably have had little effect. Households' main liability, mortgages, are now routinely securitised, which limits the impact of banking-sector problems on the availability of mortgages. Credit-card debt is also increasingly securitised, and, in any case, is one of banks' most profitable products. Indeed, overall household indebtedness continued to grow in 1990 and 1991, rising somewhat faster than disposable income. By this measure, there has been no evidence of an absolute "retrenching" in the household sector. However, from 1984 to 1989, household liabilities grew much faster than income, and a slowing of borrowing has meant that spending is now less fuelled by credit growth than in those years.

One way to measure the possible importance of household balance-sheet restructuring is to look at the saving rate. If households are paying down debt rather than spending, the saving rate will rise and consumption will fall off relative to income.[3] The data suggest some retrenching in both 1990 and 1991, as the saving rate rose from 4.0 in 1989 to 4.4 per cent in 1990 and again to 4.7 per cent in 1991. Hence, the unwillingness of households to spend appears to be playing some role in slowing the recovery.

While household liabilities expanded modestly in 1991, there was considerable change in their composition, as consumer instalment credit – largely credit-card debt and automobile loans – fell slightly over the year, while mortgage debt, especially home-equity loans, grew to offset these loans. To some extent, this could be viewed as a phenomenon that was long overdue, since credit-card interest rates have greatly exceeded mortgage interest rates for many years, and only mortgage interest has been fully deductible since the 1986 tax reform. The trend appears to have continued in the first part of 1992, as consumer credit fell still further, while mortgage debt continued to expand. Overall, this shift is encouraging, since the much-lower interest rates on mortgage debt should help improve household cash flow.

Debt reduction has been more noticeable in the business sector. Business-sector liabilities fell relative to nominal output in 1990 and 1991. Within the liabilities category, there has been a considerable shift in composition in recent years. While liabilities as a share of GDP were at about their 1987 level at the

Table 5. Household and business-sector liabilities

	1980	1981	1982	1983	1984	1985	1986	1987	1988	1989	1990	1991
Household liabilities ratio to disposable income	0.760	0.739	0.729	0.749	0.760	0.814	0.862	0.903	0.928	0.953	0.987	0.993
Mortgages	0.499	0.485	0.473	0.479	0.483	0.504	0.548	0.599	0.628	0.653	0.702	0.711
Consumer installment credit	0.155	0.145	0.142	0.150	0.163	0.179	0.186	0.188	0.190	0.193	0.184	0.176
Other	0.107	0.109	0.114	0.120	0.114	0.131	0.128	0.116	0.110	0.107	0.101	0.106
Business sector liabilities ratio to business GDP[1]	0.858	0.849	0.886	0.898	0.922	0.957	0.998	1.014	1.016	1.014	0.998	0.987
Corporate bonds	0.165	0.157	0.159	0.153	0.152	0.165	0.192	0.202	0.212	0.216	0.217	0.231
Commercial paper	0.013	0.017	0.015	0.013	0.019	0.022	0.018	0.020	0.021	0.025	0.026	0.021
Bank lending[2]	0.367	0.358	0.380	0.391	0.402	0.413	0.434	0.434	0.420	0.413	0.394	0.376
Trade debt	0.179	0.176	0.173	0.173	0.168	0.169	0.165	0.168	0.171	0.169	0.169	0.171
Other[3]	0.134	0.141	0.159	0.167	0.181	0.188	0.188	0.191	0.191	0.191	0.192	0.187

1. Excluding foreign direct investment.
2. Includes mortgages and bank lending not elsewhere classified.
3. Includes finance company loans, public lending, and other miscellaneous liabilities.
Source: Federal Reserve Board, Balance Sheets for the U.S. Economy, 1960-91.

end of 1991 (109 per cent of sector output), bank lending shrank from 39 to 35 per cent of the total and corporate bonds expanded from an 18 to a 21 per cent share; these trends were also significant in 1990. An additional factor last year was a drop in the market share of commercial paper, as firms moved to replace low-interest rate paper with high-interest rate bonds, apparently in the belief that short-term rates would eventually move above current long rates. The rapid issuance of bonds has meant that, in aggregate, credit issuance has remained positive, but most small and mid-sized firms do not have access to the bond market. For the non-corporate business sector overall, the sharp reduction in bank lending – some loan categories were down 15 per cent last year – has not been entirely offset by other sources (including finance companies), and overall liabilities were down about a percentage point in 1991. While "securitisation" seems to have left some borrowers – notably households and corporate business – largely immune from banking-sector difficulties, smaller businesses appear to remain vulnerable.

Monetary policy

Inflationary pressures have diminished considerably as a result of the 1990-91 recession and the surrounding periods of sub-par growth. As a consequence, it has been possible to ease monetary policy in order to support economic growth while at the same time making further progress toward price stability. From November 1990 to April 1991, the Federal Reserve cut short-term interest rates several times and reduced reserve requirements on certain deposits (see last year's *Survey* for more details). Altogether, the Federal funds rate fell more than 2 percentage points over this period, to below 6 per cent. By mid-1991, economic recovery appeared to be under way, and monetary easing paused for a while. During the summer, however, sluggish growth in the M2 monetary aggregate raised concerns that the recovery might have stalled, and the Fed began cutting interest rates again. By the end of the year, indicators of spending and output confirmed the impression of a renewed slowdown in growth and continued disinflationary pressures, and the Federal Reserve slashed the discount rate by a full percentage point in December. The Federal funds rate was allowed to fall again in April 1992, and on July 2, the discount rate was cut by ½ percentage point and the Federal funds rate fell by a similar amount, in response to weak M2

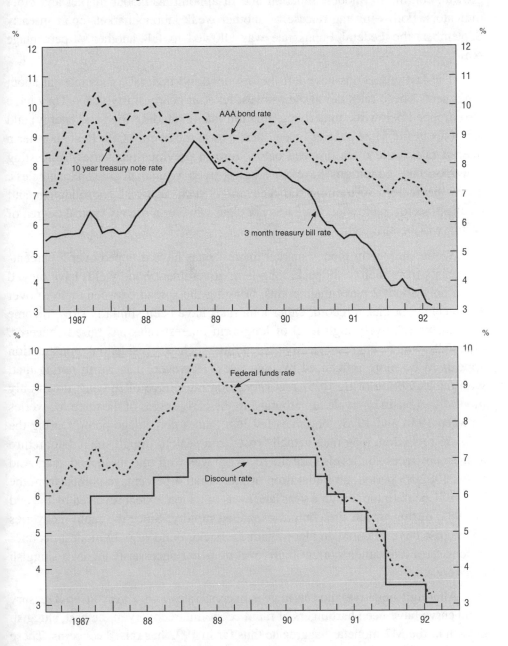

Diagram 8. **NOMINAL INTEREST RATES ARE LOW**

Source: Federal Reserve Board, *Federal Reserve Bulletin*.

growth, continuing modest inflation and disappointing labour-market and other indicators. Following the release of another weak labour-market report in early September, the Federal Funds rate was allowed to fall another ¼ percentage point.

The last reductions have left the discount and Federal Funds rates at about 3 per cent. These rates are at their lowest level in nearly thirty years. They have also dropped below the underlying inflation rate (excluding food and energy) and are at about the same pace as recent increases in the overall CPI. Real short-term interest rates have often dropped below zero in previous recoveries, suggesting that monetary conditions have now eased by a typical degree.[4] Nonetheless, given the factors restraining the recovery – such as fiscal consolidation and business-sector debt reduction – it is not clear whether a merely typical degree of easing will be sufficient.

While short-term money market interest rates have dropped over 5 percentage points from their 1989 peak, long-term government bond yields have moved down only about 2 percentage points, bringing the spread between them to over 4 percentage points, a record. Other long rates have been similarly slow to come down. This relatively high level of long-term interest rates has raised concerns, especially since interest-sensitive spending such as residential construction appears to be more influenced by long rates. However, it is worth noting that, with the exception of the 1982 recovery, long rates have often come down only modestly in business-cycle turnarounds. In the early stages of the three recoveries between 1958 and 1973, long rates fell less than a percentage point. During the 1974-75 recession, long rates actually rose from peak to trough and did not return to their pre-recession levels until the recovery was well into its second year. And in the 1982-83 period, an initial drop of more than 4 percentage points (from the late-1981 peak to the trough a year later) was to a large extent reversed by the end of 1983, during which time output expanded rapidly. Since the rapid recoveries of the past have often taken place against a background of only modest declines in long-term rates, their current high level does not necessarily signal a sluggish recovery.

Although negative short-term real interest rates and a very steep Treasury yield curve have been harbingers of rapid economic recovery in the past, sluggish growth in the M2 monetary aggregate thus far in 1992 has raised concerns. These concerns are heightened because M2 also stalled ahead of 1991's slowdown in

Diagram 9. **BANKING ACTIVITY REMAINS SLUGGISH**

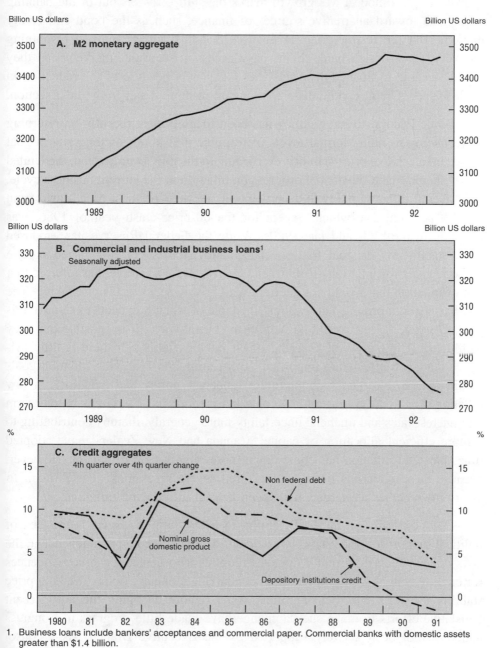

1. Business loans include bankers' acceptances and commercial paper. Commercial banks with domestic assets greater than $1.4 billion.
Source: The Federal Reserve Bank of St. Louis.

growth. In part, modest M2 growth marks the shift of assets out of the banking sector and toward alternative sources of finance, such as the bond and equity markets. But the restructuring of finances that this reflects may be restraining recovery, since not all bank clients have access to securities markets, and they may be unable to finance their activities adequately because of the reduction in bank finance. Credit conditions are discussed in more detail in the next section.

While Federal Reserve policy has been focused most recently on returning the economy to more normal levels of resource utilisation, its longer-term goal has been to achieve price stability. According to the OECD projection, the United States should make substantial progress on inflation in the current business cycle, with overall inflation likely to drop below its recent 3 per cent pace, down from the 4½ per cent rate which, except for the oil-price-crash year of 1986, was common in the mid- and late-1980s. While the Federal Reserve has espoused price stability as its goal for monetary policy, it has not established precise numeric goals for inflation – Chairman Greenspan, for example, has referred to a rate of inflation that would not interfere with private-sector decision-making. The Fed has also not provided an explicit timetable of when it expects to achieve this goal. Concrete targets would be helpful in several ways. It is possible that they would reduce the costs of bringing down inflation, although there is little evidence that such effects are important.[5] But setting and achieving inflation goals would reduce uncertainty about future monetary policy and help lock in low inflation. This reduced uncertainty could help reduce risk premiums in long-term real interest rates and financial uncertainty more generaly, thereby contributing to a more efficient allocation of capital. Canada and New Zealand have adopted timetables and inflation has come down more rapidly than called for. However, because these countries have also suffered severe recessions, it is difficult to determine whether the targets have been helpful in reducing inflation.

One constraint on the Fed's ability to adopt explicit targets is the lack of political support for price stability as a goal. Although the Fed is independent, the laws under which it currently operates requires it to consider the consequences for employment as well as inflation in conducting monetary policy. Making price stability the sole objective of policy would require changing the law. Recent legislative efforts to make such a change have made little progress in Congress and have not been actively supported by the Executive Branch. As a consequence, the Fed's inflation targets have had to remain vague.

Prospects

The economy is assumed to grow at about the same pace in the second half of 1992 as in the first half – about 2 per cent. After that, growth is expected to increase gradually, as earlier monetary easing begins to affect the economy and the private-sector factors restraining recovery – notably debt reduction – begin to be reversed. In particular, housing starts should continue to rise, and residential construction should grow at double-digit rates. Non-residential construction, a significant drag on the economy in 1991, should be less of a negative factor in 1992: investment-intentions surveys suggest that firms intend to increase capital spending fairly strongly overall this year. Inventories are very lean, and so further expenditure increases should be translated quickly into production. With productivity already back to its pre-recession trend, increased production is likely to require additional hiring, which should reassure households and contribute to their willingness to spend.

Still, the pace of recovery is expected to remain less than normal. The need for budgetary consolidation, especially at the Federal level, means that fiscal policy will be an ongoing drag on the economy: defence spending is not expected to reach 1991 levels in nominal terms until 1996. The overhang of commercial building ensures that this sector will make no contribution to growth. Monetary conditions do not appear to be sufficiently loose to completely offset these factors, since real short-term interest rates are only about as low as they have typically been in the early stages of previous recoveries.

The sluggish recovery will bring unemployment down only slowly, and the unemployment rate should still be near 7½ per cent at the end of 1993. With ample slack in labour and product markets, underlying inflation will continue to drop from its early-1992 level of around 4 per cent to below 3 per cent by the end of 1993; this pattern is somewhat obscured in overall consumer prices by movements in food and energy prices. Labour-market slack should continue beyond the projection horizon and there should be some further improvement in inflation. The projection assumes that the Fed will begin to raise rates in 1993, with a goal of achieving a "soft-landing" later in the decade.

Exports are expected to continue to grow robustly, as U.S. firms are highly competitive, given the recent depreciation of the dollar. Imports will move up again as the U.S. economy recovers, and, on balance, the U.S. goods and services

Table 6. **Near-term outlook**

Percentage change from previous period, seasonally adjusted at annual rates, volume (1987 prices)

	1987 current prices $ billion	% of GDP	1990	1991	1992	1993	1991 I	1991 II	1992 I	1992 II	1993 I	1993 II
Private consumption	3 052.2	67.2	1.2	-0.6	2.0	2.1	-1.8	1.2	2.4	2.2	1.9	2.2
Government consumption	881.6	19.4	3.3	1.2	-0.6	-0.9	3.0	-2.5	-0.2	0.0	-1.2	-1.2
Gross fixed investment	723.0	15.9	-3.1	-8.5	5.1	7.2	-13.1	-0.0	7.1	6.3	6.8	8.7
of which:												
Residential	225.2	5.0	-9.1	-12.6	12.4	9.9	-11.5	11.8	16.0	6.3	10.7	12.0
Non-residential	497.8	11.0	-0.8	-7.1	2.6	6.2	-11.3	-3.8	4.0	6.3	5.4	7.5
Final domestic demand	4 656.8	102.6	0.9	-1.4	2.0	2.2	-2.6	0.3	2.5	2.4	2.2	2.5
Stockbuilding[1]	26.3	0.6	-0.6	-0.3	0.1	0.2	-0.6	1.1	-0.3	-0.1	0.3	0.2
Total domestic demand	4 683.0	103.2	0.3	-1.8	2.1	2.4	-3.2	1.4	2.3	2.3	2.3	2.7
Exports of goods and services	364.0	8.0	8.7	5.8	5.9	6.3	4.1	10.5	4.2	5.0	6.5	7.2
Imports of goods and services	507.1	11.2	3.1	-0.1	8.2	6.3	-6.3	13.4	6.4	7.0	5.6	6.9
Foreign balance[1]	-143.1	-3.2	0.5	0.6	-0.3	-0.0	1.2	-0.4	-0.3	-0.3	0.1	-0.0
GDP at constant prices			0.8	-1.2	1.8	2.4	-2.1	1.1	2.0	2.0	2.4	2.7
GDP price deflator			4.4	4.0	2.7	2.5	4.4	2.8	2.8	2.3	2.7	2.3
GDP at current prices	4 540.0	100.0	5.3	2.8	4.5	4.9	2.2	3.9	4.9	4.3	5.2	5.1
Memorandum items												
Private consumption deflator			5.3	4.3	3.0	2.8	4.2	3.1	3.3	2.5	3.1	2.6
Unemployment rate			5.5	6.7	7.5	7.5	6.6	6.9	7.4	7.6	7.6	7.5
Household saving rate			4.5	4.9	4.9	4.9	–	–	–	–	–	–
Net lending of general government												
$ billion			-136	-193	-290	-269	–	–	–	–	–	–
Per cent of GDP			-2.5	-3.4	-4.9	-4.3	–	–	–	–	–	–
Current-account balance												
$ billion			-90	-4	-56	-70	–	–	–	–	–	–
Per cent of GDP			-1.6	-0.1	-0.9	-1.1	–	–	–	–	–	–

1. The yearly and half-yearly rates of change refer to changes expressed as a percentage of GDP in the previous period.
Source: OECD estimates.

balance should deteriorate somewhat in the next few years. Low interest rates should, however, keep U.S. investment payouts low, which will help keep down the current-account deficit. Overall, the external deficit is expected to deteriorate as the economy recovers, but will not far exceed 1 per cent of GDP.

The major upside risk to the projection is that the recovery will take on a more normal character and growth will pick up sooner and to a greater extent than projected. Business-cycle dynamics are not well understood, and it is possible that the reinforcing cycle of inventories, employment and consumer spending may operate independently of the particular constellation of monetary and structural factors that the OECD projection assumes will restrain output growth. Of course, if this is the case, monetary policy will need to begin to tighten sooner and more forcefully than assumed. The main downside risk is that structural weaknesses may prove to be more severe and long-lived than the projection assumes. In particular, high debt levels may make households and firms unwilling to borrow and banks unwilling to lend. These factors could mean some further period of stagnation and prolonged economic hardships. But such stagnation would have the benefit of lower inflation, bringing closer the day when the book can be closed on a quarter-century of attempts to contain inflation and remove it as a factor in economic planning and decisions.

II.   Selected medium-term issues

While cyclical recovery is under way in the United States, medium-term trends are less promising. Productivity growth in the 1980s remained at the disappointing pace of the 1970s, and the investment share of output trended downward. Real wages over the decade were flat or falling, depending on the measure. Per capita consumption growth was maintained, but at the expense of falling saving rates and rising labour-force participation, trends which cannot be expected to continue. Also, low saving rates indicate that living standards in the 1980s were maintained at the expense of those in the future. This chapter reviews some of the major trends in these variables; policies that may address some of the concerns raised here are reviewed in the remaining chapters.

The threat to living standards

Living standards as measured by real per capita consumer spending rose at a $1^3/_4$ per cent annual rate in the 1980s, a modest decline from the $2^1/_4$ per cent pace of the 1970s.[5] But this growth masks serious erosion of the factors underpinning current and future living standards. First, consumer spending growth ran ahead of disposable income growth and the saving rate fell, so that consumption was to some extent maintained by reducing provisions for the future. As will be documented below, this situation looks even worse if government saving is taken into account. Second, as real hourly compensation was flat over the decade, the growth of labour income was sustained by rising labour-force participation. While increased participation boosts income, it comes at the cost of either leisure or household production, which can be thought of as unmeasured reductions in living standards. Finally, the low personal saving rate suggests that property income, which held up well in the 1980s, could be weaker in the future, while

Table 7. **Living standards and their determinants**

Average annual growth rates, unless otherwise noted

	1959-69	1969-79	1979-89
Consumer expenditures per capita, 1987 dollars	2.8	2.2	1.8
Disposable income per capita, 1987 dollars	2.9	2.2	1.5
End-of-period saving rate	6.5	7.1	4.4
Employment-to-population ratio	0.4	0.3	0.5
End-of-period level	58.0	59.9	63.0
Hourly compensation, 1987 dollars [1]	2.5	1.2	0.0
Output per hour, 1987 dollars [1]	2.4	1.3	0.8

1. Non-farm business sector.
Source: Bureau of Economic Analysis, Bureau of Labor Statistics.

large budget deficits suggest that the future burden of taxation is likely to be heavier than currently.

Productivity and investment

The U.S. statistical agencies are in the midst of revising various productivity measures, and a fully consistent set of statistics was not yet available at the time the draft *Survey* was finalised. By one standard measure – non-farm business-sector productivity in fixed 1987 prices – output per hour grew only 0.8 per cent per year in the 1980s, a further deceleration from the already anaemic 1.3 per cent pace of the 1970s. To some extent, this may reflect the increasing share of the services sector, where productivity and productivity growth traditionally have been lower and harder to measure. Data which are needed to examine the contribution of capital are available only in 1982 prices, and with these data, output per hour grew about as fast in the 1980s as in the 1970s, at a bit more than 1 per cent per year; this difference is mostly due to the base year chosen, and once revised, these data should show a similar deceleration in the 1980s. Most of the slowdown in labour productivity since the 1950s and 1960s has been the result of a reduction in total factor productivity growth rather than an important decline in the contribution of capital. Indeed, rates of increase in total factor productivity over the past twenty years are less than a third of those in the previous twenty. But more recently, slowing increases in the stock of capital, relative to labour or output, has meant that its contribution to labour productivity growth is lower than its average over the previous three decades.[6]

One measure of investment trends is the ratio of business investment to GDP in nominal dollars.[7] By this measure, the investment ratio trended downward over the 1980s. Investment based on fixed 1987 prices did better, staying about even as a ratio to GDP. Looking at net capital formation overall, the United States had the lowest investment ratio among all OECD countries in the second half of the 1980s, at about 5 per cent, compared with an OECD average of more than 8 per cent. One reason for the relatively low U.S. investment ratio is that investment goods are about 12 per cent cheaper in the United States than in other OECD countries. But even after making this adjustment, the United States remains among the lowest-investing OECD countries. Another reason it may have a low investment ratio is that it is already one of the most developed of OECD countries – indeed, as measured by purchasing-power-parity-adjusted per capita GDP, the United States is at the top. As a result, the return on investment is likely to be lower than elsewhere. For these reasons, a relatively low U.S. investment ratio is not surprising.

Private capital intensity is not the only factor contributing to labour-productivity growth. Two other factors that have been studied are the public-sector capital stock and education. The contribution of public-sector capital to growth can be calculated in a manner similar to that used to measure the contribution of private-sector capital, if it is assumed that public-sector capital earns, for example, the same return as private-sector capital. (This is a somewhat heroic assumption, since public-sector investment rarely has to pass the kinds of market tests that private-sector capital must.) Looking at the contribution of public-sector capital to growth under this assumption suggests that falling public-sector investment has had a noticeable impact on productivity growth, trimming perhaps $1/3$ percentage point from the growth rate achieved before 1970.[8]

Calculating the contribution of education to productivity growth involves perhaps even greater difficulties than those presented by public-sector capital. One recent estimate, by Jorgenson and Fraumeni (1991), measures the contribution of human capital to growth using estimated contributions to earnings of additional education. This measure suggests that while the contribution of education may have dropped from the 1950s to the 1970s, it picked back up again in

Diagram 10. **U.S. SAVING AND INVESTMENT ARE
THE LOWEST IN THE OECD**

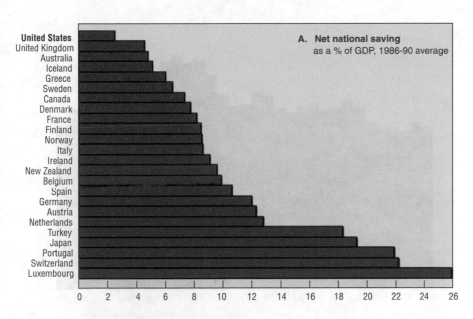

A. **Net national saving**
as a % of GDP, 1986-90 average

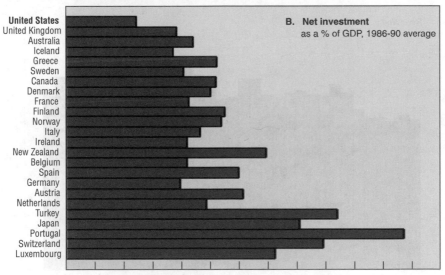

B. **Net investment**
as a % of GDP, 1986-90 average

Source: OECD, *National Accounts.*

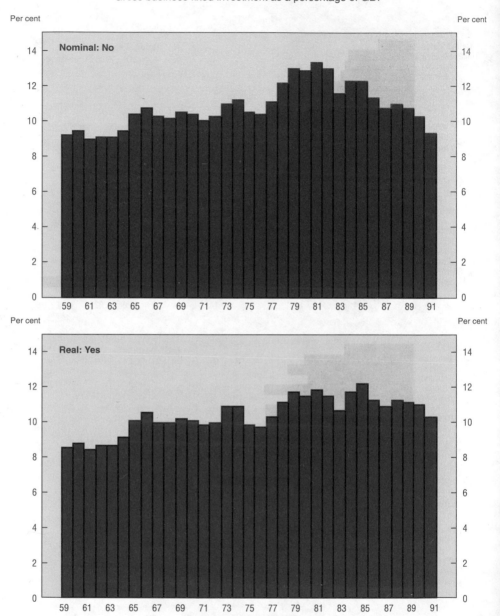

Diagram 11. **DID INVESTMENT HOLD UP IN THE 1980s?**

Gross business fixed investment as a percentage of GDP

Source: Department of Commerce, *Survey of Current Business.*

Table 8. **Explaining productivity growth**

Private non-farm business sector
Average annual percentage changes, 1982 dollars

	1949-59	1959-69	1969-79	1979-89
Output per hour	2.7	2.5	1.2	1.1
of which:				
Contribution of capital	0.8	0.9	0.7	0.5
Multifactor productivity	1.9	1.6	0.5	0.6
Capital per hour	2.4	2.7	2.6	1.9
Possible factors explaining multifactor productivity[1]				
Government capital[2]	0.4	0.4	0.2	0.0
Education[3]	0.4	0.1	0.0	0.4
Final residual	1.1	1.1	0.3	0.2
Memorandum				
Output per hour, 1987 dollars		2.4	1.3	0.8

1. Not fully consistent with the figures above and should be taken as suggestive only.
2. Based on calculations in the *1989-90 OECD Economic Survey of the United States.*
3. Based on calculations in Jorgenson and Fraumeni (1991).
Source: Except as noted, Bureau of Labor Statistics.

the 1980s. By this particular measure, it appears that expenditures have been sufficient to maintain education's contribution to growth.[9] (Another element of human capital – experience – may also have held down productivity growth in recent decades. As the labour force participation rate of women rose substantially over this period, these new entrants to the labour force may have had lower levels of productivity due to their lack of experience.) Together, the measures of government capital and educational investment used here contributed less to productivity growth over the most recent twenty-year period than over the previous two decades. However, they account for less than half of total factor productivity growth and account for only 1/4 of the slowdown in productivity growth. Most of the slowdown remains unexplained.

The recent "new growth theory" suggests that the standard method used here to decompose total factor productivity may underestimate the impact of human and private and public physical capital on growth. This would be true if there are increasing returns to scale or externalities associated with education or physical capital. Empirical evidence is mixed. Baily and Schultze (1990) find little evidence that the share of physical capital understates the impact of capital on growth for the U.S. economy over time, while Englander and Mittelstädt (1988) find a positive relationship between total factor productivity growth and investment across OECD countries. It is worth pointing out that the current size of such additional effects cannot be very large, since the recent unexplained productivity residual for the United States is itself not very large.[10]

Real wages and salaries

While productivity growth has been disappointing, real wages and salaries have not been able to do even this well. Real wages and salaries, depending on the measure used, have either just managed to stay level or have fallen. Indeed, one of the most-cited measures of wages – real average hourly earnings of production workers – has declined 7 per cent over the past decade, while another measure – real compensation of all workers – was unchanged between 1979 and 1989. Certainly from the standpoint of living standards of many American workers, this is alarming.

One part of the divergence between labour-productivity and real-wage growth has been changes in the share of income going to capital. Labour's share dropped on average 0.3 per cent per year in the 1980s, reversing the gains made in the 1960s and 1970s. One reason the share of income going to capital may have risen is the higher level of real interest rates in the 1980s. While capital income obviously also contributes to the ability to sustain living standards, the distributional consequences are different, since capital income goes to a much larger extent to high-income people than does labour income.[11]

The growth rates of real wages and productivity also diverged because consumer prices rose more quickly than product prices. This largely reflects the fact that prices of investment goods rose less rapidly than did prices of consumer goods and services. To the extent that workers save, they also benefit from the smaller increases in investment prices. However, real wages are traditionally measured with respect to consumption prices only.

Two factors that help explain the better performance of hourly compensation relative to average hourly earnings are that the latter excludes non-wage benefits and that it covers only production workers, and so excludes more highly paid supervisory and managerial employees. A measure of the impact of benefits

Table 9. **Why has productivity grown faster than real wages?**

Average annual percentage changes

Unless otherwise noted, real wages are deflated by the consumer price index

	1959-69	1969-79	1979-89
Output per hour [1]	2.4	1.3	0.8
Product-based real compensation per hour, all workers [1]	2.5	1.5	0.5
Real compensation/hour, all workers	2.5	1.2	0.0
Real average hourly earnings, production workers	1.8	0.2	−0.7
Memorandum			
ECI-based data [2] (private industry workers)			
Real compensation/hour, all workers			0.1
Real wage, all workers			−0.3
Real wage, production workers			−0.3

1. Non-farm business sector, 1987 dollars.
2. Data reflects December of each year.
Source: Bureau of Labor Statistics.

can be found from the difference between wage and compensation growth for all workers: costs of employer-paid benefits – especially for medical insurance – rose more rapidly than wages in the 1980s, while real wages excluding benefits fell in real terms. The remaining discrepancy appears to be the result of shifts in the composition of employment, although because data sources differ, measurement error may also play a role.[12]

Saving and the current account

As well as having the lowest investment ratio, the United States is also the lowest-saving country in the OECD, and its saving ratio has trended downward in the 1980s. In the second half of the 1980s, for example, the net national saving rate was 2½ per cent of GDP in the United States – a decline from 7 per cent in the 1970s – compared with an average for the rest of the OECD of more than 10 per cent. Both public and private saving contributed to the drop in overall national saving; private saving fell by a bit more than 2 percentage points of GDP, while the public sector accounted for another 1½ percentage points. Higher

Table 10. Saving and investment trends

As a percentage of GDP

	1961-65	1966-70	1971-75	1976-80	1981-85	1986-90
Capital formation	15.9	15.9	16.4	18.1	17.4	16.0
Business investment	10.5	11.7	11.4	12.8	13.2	11.4
Residential investment	5.1	4.2	5.0	5.3	4.2	4.6
National saving	16.7	16.2	16.7	17.6	16.2	13.7
Government saving	–0.2	–0.5	–1.2	–0.8	–2.9	–2.4
Federal	–0.2	–0.5	–1.8	–1.9	–4.1	–3.2
State and local	0.0	0.1	0.6	1.1	1.2	0.8
Private saving	16.9	16.7	17.9	18.3	19.1	16.1
Business saving	12.3	11.6	11.9	13.3	13.5	12.7
Household saving	4.6	5.1	6.0	5.1	5.7	3.4
Statistical discrepancy	–0.2	0.0	0.2	0.5	–0.0	–0.2
Net foreign investment	0.9	0.4	0.5	0.0	–1.2	–2.5
Memorandum						
Net capital formation	7.1	7.5	7.0	7.4	5.5	5.0
Net saving	8.2	7.8	7.3	6.9	4.3	2.7

Note: Data may not add due to rounding.
Source: Department of Commerce, *Survey of Current Business.*

Table 11. Saving based on changes in assets

Average change in end-of-year net worth as percentage of disposable income

	1961-65	1966-70	1971-75	1976-80	1981-85	1986-90
Nominal						
Total	27.6	28.2	35.1	53.8	27.2	21.8
Households	29.1	30.1	38.0	56.5	33.6	28.0
Public	–1.5	–1.9	–2.9	–2.8	–6.3	–6.2
Real[1]						
Total	20.7	12.0	9.4	22.6	6.5	3.9
Households	21.2	12.0	9.6	22.4	10.9	7.7
Public	–0.5	0.0	–0.2	0.2	–4.5	–3.8
Memorandum						
Ratios to disposable income						
Total net worth	4.5	4.4	4.2	4.4	4.3	4.3
Household net worth	5.2	5.0	4.7	4.8	4.7	4.9

1. End-of-year asset levels are deflated by the fourth-quarter personal consumption deflator. Annual average disposable income
   is deflated by the annual average of the personal consumption deflator.
Source: Federal Reserve Board, *Flow of Funds Accounts;* Department of Commerce, *Survey of Current Business.*

Federal government budget deficits were the main public-sector drain on national saving.

Asset-based measures also show a drop-off in saving from the 1960s and 1970s to the 1980s.[13] For total assets, the average real saving rate dropped from 16 per cent in the 1960s and 1970s to about 5 per cent in the 1980s. For overall household assets, the drop-off is somewhat less severe, with a drop of only 5 percentage points, to about 9 per cent of disposable income per year. However, much of the accumulation of household assets was in the form of government debt, which was accumulated, in real terms, at about 4 per cent per year in the 1980s, after being about flat in the previous two decades. Here again, the drop in government saving accounts for a bit less than half the overall reduction in saving.

Free international flow of capital has meant that the United States has been able to have an investment rate exceeding its saving rate by running a current-account deficit. From a theoretical perspective, a secular current-account deficit for a rich country like the United States could be considered both unusual and undesirable. Because the United States is already highly advanced, it has a high capital-labour ratio, and, all else equal, the return to further investment should be comparatively low. The United States' low investment ratio is not inconsistent with this. As a result, one might expect the United States to be, on average, a net supplier of capital to the rest of the world. But since the United States has a much lower saving rate than other countries, it ran large current-account deficits through much of the 1980s. More recently, these deficits have diminished sub-stantially but, aside from the special transfers associated with the Gulf War, the improvement has to a greater extent reflected reduced investment than increased saving.

Because the United States has such a large economy, persistent and large current-account deficits can pose a drain on world resources large enough to have a significant effect on world real interest rates and world investment, which ultimately means reduced investment in the United States itself. As well, the deficits have provided cover for domestic advocates of protectionism, potentially weakening the United States' traditional support for free trade. If the low overall domestic saving rate were entirely attributable to private saving, then perhaps it could be dismissed as a private-sector decision that, aside from the possible need for reforms to remove distortions, was of little concern to policy makers. But the increase in the Federal budget deficit has been, in an accounting sense, one of the main sources of lower saving over the 1980s. The benefits to be gained from addressing the deficit problem could be substantial; for example, the average Federal deficit in the late 1980s was larger than the net national saving rate and larger than the net inflow of foreign capital (Table 9). Thus, even if there were some offsets in private-sector behaviour, eliminating the late 1980s Federal deficit would have nearly doubled the national saving rate and left the United States as a net contributor to global capital markets, as might generally be expected for a wealthy country.[14]

III. Federal fiscal policy over the medium term

The budget deficit in the United States remains a significant problem. The Federal deficit for fiscal year 1992 is projected at about 5½ per cent of GDP, and even abstracting from the influence of the business cycle and other transitory factors (such as deposit insurance), estimates of the structural Federal deficit remain at about 3 per cent of GDP. Deficits of this size eat up more than half of net private saving. Low U.S. saving threatens future living standards, and, because the U.S. economy is so large, forces up world interest rates. Various attempts to reduce the structural deficit have not been successful. Previous approaches – including the recent Budget Enforcement Act and the earlier Gramm-Rudman laws – have focused mainly on procedure and to that extent have not made the legislative changes necessary to bring spending under control. Future efforts at deficit reduction need to focus more on making changes to taxes and specific programmes – such as spending on health care – that will allow spending to be controlled. While the 1990 Budget Act included such measures, further actions are needed. This chapter begins by outlining trends in spending and revenue and then discusses recent procedures to control the deficit as well as sources of deficit over-shooting. The chapter ends with a discussion of some specific spending and tax proposals.

An overview of government spending and revenue trends

For the public sector as a whole, budget deficits widened considerably in the 1980s. Most of this widening has been the tresult of larger Federal government deficits, as the state and local surplus has, until the recent recession, been fairly stable. Mechanically, the expansion of the Federal deficit since the 1960s is the product of spending that has outstripped tax revenues. Based on national-accounts data, revenues have been around 19 or 20 per cent of GDP since the late

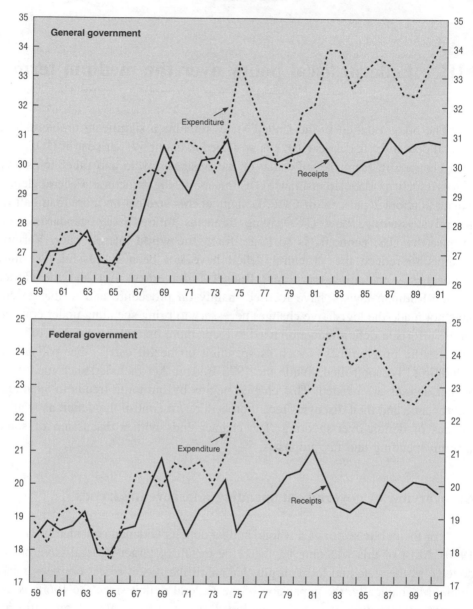

Diagram 12.   **GOVERNMENT SPENDING, REVENUES AND DEFICITS**
National accounts basis
Per cent of GDP

General government

Expenditure

Receipts

Federal government

Expenditure

Receipts

Source: Department of Commerce, *Survey of Current Business.*

Table 12.   **Federal government spending and revenues**

National accounts basis
Per cent of GDP

	1961-65	1966-70	1971-75	1976-80	1981-85	1986-90
Revenue						
Indirect taxes	2.5	2.0	1.6	1.3	1.6	1.2
Corporate taxes	4.0	3.7	3.0	3.0	1.9	2.1
Social security	3.8	4.9	6.0	6.7	7.5	7.9
Individual taxes	8.1	8.8	8.5	8.8	8.9	8.6
Total	18.5	19.5	19.2	19.8	19.9	19.9
Expenditure						
Non-defence purchases	2.4	2.3	2.4	2.4	2.2	2.0
Defence purchases	8.3	8.4	6.0	5.1	6.1	6.1
Transfers	4.8	5.4	7.7	8.8	9.7	9.1
Subsidies	0.5	0.5	0.5	0.4	0.5	0.5
Grants-in-aid	1.5	2.1	3.0	3.4	2.6	2.3
Net interest	1.2	1.3	1.3	1.6	2.8	3.1
Total	18.7	20.0	21.0	21.7	24.0	23.1
Deficit	–0.2	–0.5	–1.8	–1.9	–4.1	–3.2

Source: Department of Commerce, *Survey of Current Business.*

1960s, while spending rose from 20 per cent of GDP in the late 1960s to a peak around 24 per cent in the mid-1980s, before moving down to about 23 per cent from 1987 to 1991.

The increase in spending has been largely due to transfers and net interest payments. Most of the increase in transfers had occurred by the early 1980s: spending under the Social Security programme (mostly old-age pensions) as a share of GDP, for example, peaked above 5 per cent in 1983, before edging down to its present range of between 4$\frac{1}{2}$ and 4$\frac{3}{4}$ per cent of GDP. Most of the increase in Medicare (the programme for health care of the elderly) as a share of GDP had also occurred by the mid-1980s, although recently a surge in physician costs has pushed this share higher again. Means-tested transfers – to poor people – reached a plateau of about 1$\frac{3}{4}$ per cent of GDP by the mid-1970s, although here again, rising medical costs have recently led to an increased GDP share. As spending had moved significantly ahead of receipts by the early 1980s, net interest payments picked up, moving from less than 2 per cent of GDP in the late 1970s to 3$\frac{1}{2}$ per cent by 1991.

51

In contrast, government purchases of goods and services have been trending down relative to GDP since the late 1960s. Between 1969 and 1979, defence spending dropped by 4 percentage points of GDP, to about 5 per cent. There was a surge of defence spending in the mid-1980s which brought its level above 6 per cent of GDP, but this has since been largely reversed. On current prospects, defence spending is set to decline even more. On a national-accounts basis, non-defence purchases came down by about 1/2 per cent of GDP during the 1980s to about 2 per cent.

While tax revenue has remained fairly stable as a share of GDP in recent years, its composition has changed considerably. Indirect taxes – such as excise taxes on gasoline, cigarettes and alcohol – have fallen off substantially as a revenue source, as have corporate taxes. Indirect taxes fell from 2$\frac{1}{2}$ per cent of GDP in the early 1960s to only 1 per cent of GDP by the late 1980s; however, they moved up a bit since 1990 as a result of the Budget Enforcement Act. Corporate profits tax receipts have dropped from around 4 per cent of GDP in the 1960s to around 2 per cent more recently. Most of the offsetting increase in revenues has come from the Social Security and other payroll taxes, which have more than doubled as a share of GDP, from 3$\frac{3}{4}$ per cent in the early 1960s to nearly 8 per cent recently. Receipts from the individual income tax have varied from just below 8 to just over 9 per cent of GDP since the late 1960s.

Although overall government expenditures as a share of GDP were at a historical high in the 1980s, the United States still has relatively low public spending in comparison with other OECD countries. Indeed, counting all levels of government, only Turkey, Japan and Australia spend less as a share of GDP than does the United States. And, except for Turkey, the United States is also the most lightly taxed, with just 32 per cent of GDP going to the government in 1989; indeed, it would remain among the least taxed even if taxes were raised sufficiently to balance the Federal budget.

One reason the U.S. government expenditure share is low relative to other OECD countries is the comparatively high private-sector share of health expenditures. If a more-typical fraction of overall health-care costs were covered by the government (say, 80 per cent), the 1989 share of government spending in GDP would have been 38 per cent, slightly below the OECD average of 41 per cent.

Diagram 13. THE U.S. HAS LOW TAXES AND SPENDING

General government spending and receipts

As a percentage of GDP, 1989[1]

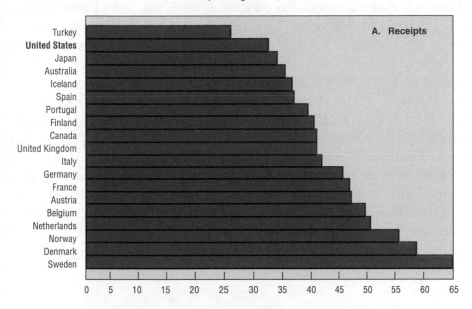

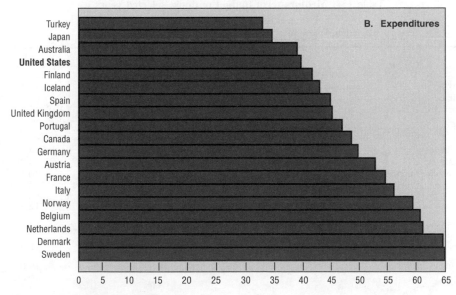

1. For Spain the percentages are for 1988.
Source: OECD, *National Accounts.*

What are the medium-term prospects for the Federal budget deficit? According to estimates from the Congressional Budget Office (CBO, 1992c), the structural deficit is currently around 3¹/₂ per cent of GDP and, under current legislation, is not likely to drop below 3 per cent through the middle of the decade. Revenues are expected to stay near their recent level of 19 per cent of GDP, and spending at 22 per cent. Within spending, though, the composition is projected to change substantially. The United States is expected to continue to benefit from a "peace dividend" – cuts of about 2 per cent of GDP in defence spending by 1996 – but spending under existing transfer programmes, according to CBO estimates, is expected to rise enough to offset these declines (CBO, 1992c). The bulk of the increases is projected to go to health care for the elderly. After 1995, the restraint from the peace dividend expires, and the underlying spending pressures from rising health-care costs are projected to lead to further increases in the ratio of the structural deficit to GDP, possibly exceeding 5 per cent early in the next decade.

Table 13. **Medium-term budget outlook, selected years**

Budget basis; per cent of GDP
Excluding deposit insurance outlays and Desert Storm receipts

	1988	1991	1996
Outlays	22.0	23.1	22.1
Defense	6.0	5.7	3.8
Other discretionary	3.7	3.8	3.8
Total discretionary	9.7	9.5	7.6
Social security	4.5	4.7	4.9
Health benefits	2.4	2.9	4.2
Farm price supports	0.3	0.2	0.1
Other mandatory	3.1	3.5	3.2
Total mandatory	10.3	11.3	12.4
Net interest	3.2	3.5	3.6
Balancing amount	–1.2	–1.1	–1.0
Revenues	19.0	18.7	19.0
Deficit	3.0	4.4	3.6

Source: Congressional Budget Office (1992a, c).

A stable debt-to-GDP ratio is indicative of a sustainable fiscal policy. According to CBO estimates, the large projected deficits mean that this ratio will rise steadily, from about 48 per cent of GDP at the end of 1991, to 63 per cent ten years later. All of this comes before the surge in retirees in the early part of the next century, which, with current benefit and tax levels under the social security programme, will lead to a further increase in the deficit. Of course, such long-term projections are fraught with uncertainty.

In addition to external considerations (discussed in the previous chapter) and sustainability, a third concern raised by budget deficits is intergenerational equity. Recently, "generational accounts" have been developed which measure the present value of future taxes estimated to be paid by a generation, minus the present value of future transfers from the government which that generation is projected to receive. According to generational accounts presented in the 1993 Budget, future U.S. generations are projected to pay 79 per cent more in taxes, net of transfers they receive, than the generation born in 1990.[15] This inequity largely reflects the fast growth of Medicare and Medicaid transfers over the next few decades. Hence, sustained budget deficits are a symptom of generational inequality in U.S. fiscal policy. On the other hand, in the absence of the 1990 Budget Enforcement Act and associated Omnibus Budget Reconciliation Act, the generational gap would have been higher still, with future generations paying 97 per cent more than the 1990 cohort.

Previous attempts at deficit control

The large deficits of recent years have occurred despite repeated attempts to legislate deficit control. This section reviews some of the recent history of these attempts and some of the factors behind their failure.

Beginning in 1986, the deficit was, in principle, governed by the Gramm-Rudman-Hollings (GRH) deficit-control law.[16] This set deficit targets from 1986 until 1993, mandating a balanced budget from 1993 onwards. For the purposes of GRH, the "deficit" was defined to include the social-security surplus and deposit-insurance outlays. The actual deficit figures in Table 14 therefore include these items. The GRH targets were to be enforced by "sequesters" – mechanical reductions in expenditures according to rules laid out in the law – although loopholes were used to avoid the worst consequences of this procedure. The

Table 14. **Gramm-Rudman-Hollings targets**

$ billion, fiscal years

	1986	1987	1988	1989	1990	1991	1992	1993
GRH-1[1]	172	144	108	72	36	0	0	0
GRH-2[2]	172	144	144	136	100	64	28	0
Actual deficit	221	150	155	154	220	269		

1. Passed in 1985.
2. Passed in 1987.
Source: Budget of the United States Government, various years.

original GRH targets were greatly overrun, and in 1987 they were revised upwards, with a balanced budget required by 1993. By mid-1990, however, the Administration was contemplating a sequester of $100 billion in order to meet the GRH targets.

This unacceptable prospect brought the GRH process to a close and resulted in the 1990 Budget Enforcement Act (BEA), which was signed into law in early November 1990. It specified that the deficit was to be reduced by about $160 billion by 1995, from a baseline that was less clearly defined than (but in fact much higher than) the GRH baseline. Unlike the GRH law, the Budget Act put into place a substantial portion (about $100 billion) of the cuts "up front".

It changed the budget process in many other ways as well. Most importantly, the BEA does not set deficit targets for 1991-93. Instead, it prohibits legislated deficit increases, from mandatory spending increases or tax cuts, over a baseline that is adjusted for changes to economic conditions (slower growth, for example, will raise the baseline) and for so-called "technical" assumptions (for instance, the projected revenue from a tax). One implication of the adjustments for technical assumptions is that fluctuations in deposit-insurance outlays escape control of the Act. Discretionary spending is limited by explicit ceilings. Unlike GRH, the social-security surplus also is outside the purview of the Act, although special rules apply to it.

In view of their important role in the budgetary projections, it is worth dwelling on the nature of the so-called technical assumptions. In order to project future tax revenues and expenditures on mandatory spending programmes,[17] assumptions are made about such things as tax elasticities and eligibility for federal benefits. These are the technical assumptions. Under the Budget Enforcement Act, the Office of Management and Budget (OMB, the arm of the Administration responsible for the Budget) must choose its technical assumptions five days after a tax or expenditure bill has been signed into law. Subsequent revisions to technical assumptions change the projected baseline deficit but will not trigger sequesters under the BEA. In the OMB mid-session review of July 1991, for example, projected tax revenue was reduced by about $20 billion per year because of changed technical assumptions (in part, this was the result of correcting an error in the Treasury's tax model), and expenditures were revised up by $5 to $15 billion per year because of higher projected Medicaid expenditures.

The BEA does control legislated changes to taxes and expenditures. For example, a legislated extension of Medicaid benefits would have to be matched either by equal cuts in other mandatory programmes or by higher taxes. The nature of the control (called "pay-as-you-go") is complicated, but its effect is to prevent legislation from raising the deficit above the baseline. The substantial upward revisions to the deficit since late 1990 have not contravened the Act (although two tiny sequesters have been triggered under the Act). Finally, it should be noted that the caps on discretionary spending under the BEA imply real spending cuts in this category.

While the BEA has not sufficed to eliminate budgetary pressures, it represents a marked improvement over GRH in various respects. First, "pay-as-you-go" restrictions provide more explicit guidance to lawmakers to restrict deficit expansion than deficit ceilings alone. Second, because BEA targets can be changed in response to changes in the economy and technical assumptions, the BEA law is more resilient with respect to deficit "surprises"; each time the GRH law was re-written in response to unsustainable deficit pressures, extra spending was allowed. Third, this resiliency under the BEA allows a counter-cyclical movement in the deficit that would not be permitted under GRH. Finally, the spending cuts and tax increases associated with the BEA also had significant effects in lowering the deficit below what it otherwise would be. The BEA is described in greater detail in last year's *Survey*.

Deficit projections and outcomes

Table 15 shows the recent history of deficit outcomes, and of projections by the OMB, the Congressional Budget Office (CBO) and the OECD Secretariat (which relies heavily on the CBO projection). Both the OMB and the CBO publish two estimates each year, one connected with the Budget early in the year, and a mid-year update (only the OMB update is shown in Table 15). This table shows the "total", or "consolidated", Federal deficit, which comes close to the actual net borrowing requirement the Federal government for all purposes during the fiscal year. It includes both the social-security surplus and net deposit-insurance outlays, neither of which fall under the primary control of the Budget Act.

Reading down the columns of Table 15, the 1990 deficit, which turned out to be $220 billion, was underpredicted by as much as $60 billion (by the CBO). In early 1990, the Administration predicted a 1991 deficit of only $121 billion, $148 billion lower than the outcome of $269 billion. A year later, however, the Administration's February 1991 projection was somewhat higher than the outcome.

For 1992, the Administration projected a deficit of only $44 billion in its Budget of early 1990. This forecast should, however, be regarded as artificial because the rules of the game required the projection to conform with the hopelessly optimistic GRH targets. Even so, the CBO projection, which was under no such constraint, was only $124 billion. A year later, both the OMB and the CBO had raised their projections to just under $300 billion. Six months after that, in July 1991, the OMB projection increased by some $75 billion to about $350 billion. (Although it is not shown, the CBO had raised its mid-year projection by about the same amount.) The most recent Administration projection, contained in the 1992 Mid-Session Review, is a deficit of about $334 billion. Although the 1992 Budget (released in February 1991) had predicted a small surplus in 1996, no institution is now projecting surpluses in the foreseeable future.

Table 15. **Deficit projections**

$ billion, fiscal years

	1989	1990	1991	1992	1993	1994	1995
OMB 1991 Budget							
(February 1990)[1]	154[2]	184	121	44	21	–5	–31
CBO baseline							
(March 1990)	..	159	161	124	132	121	110
EO47							
(June 1990)	..	169	163	117			
OMB mid-session review							
(July 1990)	..	218	231	205	135	80	77
EO48							
(December 1990)	..	220	243	241			
OMB 1992 Budget							
(February 1991)	..	220[2]	318	281	202	62	3
CBO baseline							
(March 1991)	..	..	309	294	221	169	69
EO49							
(July 1991)	..	..	309	278			
OMB mid-session review							
(July 1991)	..	..	282	348	246	132	74
EO50							
(December 1991)	..	..	269	374	273		
OMB 1993 Budget							
(February 1992)	..	..	269[2]	399	352	211	
CBO baseline							
(March 1992)				372	332	277	214
EO51							
(July 1992)				362	320		
OMB mid-session review							
(July 1992)				333	341	274	218

Note: OMB refers to the Office of Management and Budget (i.e. the Administration). CBO refers to the Congressional Budget Office.
1. This is the Gramm-Rudman-Hollings baseline adjusted for "outlay anomalies" and net deposit insurance costs plus the OMB's "high need" (i.e. pessimistic) projection of deposit insurance working capital.
2. Actual.
Source: Budget of the United States Government, various years, and Congressional Budget Office, *The Economic and Budget Outlook,* various years.

The sources of revision to the OMB projections of the 1991 and 1992 deficits

The Table shows the revisions to the Administration's deficit projections, as expressed in Budgets, published each February, and OMB mid-session reviews, published each July.

Sources of revisions to OMB deficit projections: 1991 and 1992

$ billion, fiscal years

	1991	1992
Revision		
February to July 1990	110	161
Deposit insurance	35	70
Technical	50	58
Economic	24	30
Law	2	2
July 1990 to February 1991	79	80
Deposit insurance	48	47
All other[1]	31	33
February to July 1991	−36	67
Deposit insurance	−28	30
Technical[2]	−9	40
Economic	−1	−3
Law	2	0
July 1991 to February 1992	−13	51
Deposit insurance	−17	−38
All other[1]	4	89

1. The Budget document gives no finer breakdown.
2. This line includes items related to Desert Storm, which resulted in a $33 billion smaller deficit for 1991, but a $12 billion larger deficit for 1992.

OMB's pessimistic deposit insurance projection is used here to calculate its February 1990 projection of the total deficit. In its mid-term review of July 1990, the OMB used a lower figure, and therefore attributed $55 billion of the revision to deposit insurance.

Revision 1: between the 1991 Budget (presented in February 1990) and the mid-session review six months later

The OMB projection of the *1991 deficit* increased by $110 billion. The largest contributor (about $50 billion) was "technical" adjustments, which reduced income and corporate tax revenues and raised outlay estimates, roughly equally. Next in importance was a re-estimate of deposit insurance outlays of $35 billion. An upward revision to the interest rate outlook added $10 billion to projected expenditures, and other changes to the economic outlook accounted for another $14 billion. Only about $2 billion was attributed to changes in laws and administrative action.

(continued on next page)

(continued)

The OMB projection for the *1992 deficit* was revised up by $161 billion. Of this, deposit insurance re-estimates accounted for $70 billion. Another $58 billion was technical, about two-thirds of which was higher expenditures. Economic assumptions accounted for $30 billion (about one-third was extra debt service due to higher interest rates). About $2 billion was attributed to changes in law.

Revision 2: between June 1990 and the 1992 Budget (presented in February 1991)

The OMB revised its *1991 deficit* projection by another $79 billion, to $310 billion, $48 billion of which is accounted for by deposit insurance. The rest is accounted for by a still more gloomy economic outlook and $8 billion for Desert Storm. Again, the contribution of changes to laws was tiny. The projection for the *1992 deficit* was raised by $80 billion (to $285 billion), $47 billion of which was accounted for by increased deposit insurance outlay projections.

Revision 3: between the 1992 Budget and the mid-session review in July 1991

The OMB projection of the *1991 deficit* was reduced by $36 billion, a revision that reflected offsetting factors. Projected deposit insurance expenditures fell by $28 billion, largely because difficulties in obtaining Congressional expenditure authorisation in early 1991 delayed the process of closing bankrupt institutions (therefore, this expenditure was simply shifted into 1992). Contributions from other countries for Desert Storm, not foreseen in the Budget, reduced the deficit by $33 billion. On the other hand, technical re-estimates reduced expected tax revenue by $21 billion (some of which was due to the correction of an error in the Treasury's tax model).

The projection for the *1992 deficit* was raised by $67 billion. There was a $30 billion upward revision to deposit insurance outlays, which is accounted for by the payments that were pushed back from 1991. Technical adjustments – reduced tax revenue projections (in part the result of the correction to the Treasury's tax model), upward revisions to medical insurance outlays, and some Desert Storm costs – accounted for $40 billion of the revision.

Revision 4: between the July 1991 mid-session review and the 1993 Budget (presented in February 1992)

The 1993 Budget raised the *1992 deficit* projection by another $50 billion, to about $400 billion. The projection of deposit insurance outlays fell by $38 billion. The Administration's policy proposals stayed within the Budget Act and were roughly revenue-neutral. Changes to economic assumptions, notably a downward revision to output growth, appear to have made a substantial contribution to the revision.

Curing the chronic U.S. deficit

Deficit reduction based on targets has not succeeded. To the extent that the deficit has been controlled, it is because specific taxes have been raised and spending cut. Since over the past several decades, the main source of the deficit has been spending increases – mostly on transfers to the elderly – that have outstripped tax revenues, the main issue in deficit reduction is whether transfers should be cut, paid for (through higher taxes), or offset through cuts in other spending.

The Administration's 1993 Budget included a proposal to control transfer payments through a "mandatory spending cap". Since most of the pressure on spending comes from health-care programmes, the cap would lead to strict limits on health spending. But it is not clear how such limits could be achieved without a major overhaul of the current Medicare and Medicaid programmes, since the laws governing those programmes stipulate eligibility and payment regimes. So while the mandatory-caps proposal correctly focuses attention on health-care costs and the resulting explosion in spending, it would, by itself, be inadequate to control spending.

A better approach would be to adopt a thoroughgoing reform of the U.S. health-care system that would include significant moves toward cost control. The issues involved in health-care reform, including specific proposals, are discussed in Chapter V. If an effective cost-control programme were adopted and the Federal responsibility for health-care spending were kept frozen at its 1991 level as a share of GDP, annual savings would, by 1996, amount to more than 1 per cent of GDP, or about $90 billion. It is worth noting, though, that many of the more thorough health-care reform proposals would involve a much larger government role in the health-care sector, which could have a dramatic impact on the fiscal situation.

Social Security and other retirement programmes (such as Federal employee pensions) are another large block of spending that have largely escaped cuts in the 1980s. Because they are so large, relatively modest cuts would generate large sums – a 6 per cent cut in benefits, which might be achieved, for example, by suspending cost-of-living increases for two years, would generate about $19 billion (based on CBO estimates). But even smaller reductions have proved politically difficult in the past.[18] One indirect approach to reducing benefits that could raise a comparable amount of revenue would be to treat Social Security benefits – which are now largely tax-exempt – as regular pension benefits.[19] This approach would have the advantage, relative to an across-the-board cut, of targeting the wealthier elderly, since it would operate through the income-tax system.

The spending proposals made so far focus on areas that have made large contributions to spending growth over the last twenty years. Together, these cuts comprise about 1½ per cent of GDP, about half of the estimated structural deficit.

Reducing the Chronic U.S. Budget Deficit

Proposal	1996 saving	
	$ billion	Per cent of GDP
Spending cuts		
1. Cap health spending through effective cost control (1) Goal: freeze Federal spending as a share of GDP at 1991 level (2.9 per cent)	89	1.2
2. Eliminate farm subsidies	10	.1
3. Treat Social Security as a regular pension benefit by raising taxable share to 85 per cent and eliminating the taxable income threshold	26	.4
Tax increases		
(Modest changes)		
4. Increase gasoline tax by 25 cents per gallon	23	.3
5. Add imputed rent for owner-occupied housing to the tax base[1]	64	0.9
6. Tax employer-paid health insurance	40	.5
(A bigger change)		
7. Introduce a broad-based, 5 per cent VAT	140	1.9
(By way of comparison)		
8. Change personal and corporate income tax rates:		
5 per cent income-tax surcharge	36	.5
Raise rates by 7 per cent	42	.6
Memo:		
Estimated 1996 deficit (excluding deposit insurance)	222	3.0

Source: Congressional Budget Office estimates (CBO, 1992*b*), except (1), OECD estimates.

A popular idea in the 1980s was to balance the budget by reducing "wasteful" government spending. Over the recent past and prospectively, large cuts have already been made in many areas of Federal spending – as noted, the GDP share of non-defence spending was cut by 20 per cent over the 1980s, while defence spending is to be reduced significantly in the years ahead. Means-tested spending for items other than Medicaid has been reduced significantly – by the late 1980s, spending in this area was about 1 per cent of GDP, down about 20 per cent as a share of GDP from a decade earlier. This item includes most of the traditional "welfare" programmes such as food stamps and schemes to assist poor children and disabled people. Because spending in these areas has already been cut substantially, further cuts are likely to have increasing social costs, and total spending is not very big. In contrast, Social Security, other pensions and health-care spending are large and have been relatively little affected by deficit-reduction pressures.

The decision of whether to rely more heavily on spending cuts or tax increases to reduce the deficit is largely a judgmental one. The suggested spending cuts in the health and Social Security areas are tempered by a heavy measure of political reality. Of course, similar savings could be achieved by cutting welfare spending and non-defence purchases – but that would mean cutting these by half. In the OECD's judgement, there would be less social cost involved in the consideration of other measures, including tax increases.

To the extent that revenue increases are chosen, they should be such as to be as constructive as possible. One place to begin might be gasoline and other energy taxes. As a concrete example, a 25 cents-per-gallon gasoline tax would raise $23 billion per year, based on CBO estimates. Such taxes could even be beneficial since they can amount to taxes on pollution, and therefore contribute to reducing the pollution, although such taxes would be efficient only if negative externalities from pollution, congestion and road wear exceed 32 cents per gallon, the current average of federal and state taxes.

Another relatively non-damaging revenue source would be general consumption taxes. Consumption taxes are preferable to income taxes because they create greater incentives to save and invest, an important consideration in a low-saving country such as the United States. The United States relies comparatively little on consumption taxes: it is one of the few OECD countries without a national value-added tax (VAT) or retail sales tax, for example, though most states already have substantial sales taxes. According to CBO estimates, a broad-based 5 per cent VAT could raise revenues equal to about 2 per cent of GDP once fully implemented ($140 billion in 1996), enough to eliminate two-thirds of the structural deficit.

A VAT has some disadvantages, though: it is regressive and would introduce new costly administration.[20] Most of the advantages of a VAT in terms of saving incentives could be achieved through a reform of the current income-tax system. The idea – called a "direct consumption tax" – is to tax the same tax base as the VAT (value-added) through modified versions of the current personal and corporate income taxes. Labour income could continue to be taxed through the personal income tax and could therefore be made as progressive as desired. Taxing the contribution of capital to value-added would require several modifications of the current personal and corporate income taxes: investment and capital gains would need to be dropped from the tax base, and the current double-taxation of corporate dividends would need to be eliminated.

While such changes would lead to a more sensible U.S. tax system, they would require a time-consuming, wholesale revision of the U.S. tax system. An alternative way to proceed would be to amend the tax system in ways that address current distortions while also collecting more revenue. One large current distortion is the lack of any tax on the implicit rent from owner-occupied housing, which leads to an excessive housing stock and inadequate business capital. To some extent, state and local property levies serve as taxes on these rents. But the best way to tax this implicit rent would be to add it directly to the income tax base. A rough calculation suggests that this might raise 0.9 per cent of GDP in tax revenue.[21] However, estimating imputed rents would be difficult, and adding a tax is likely to prove disruptive to housing and financial markets, since house prices would probably tumble as a result. Even capturing a portion of these rents, though, could make a significant contribution to deficit reduction and greater economic efficiency.

Some other tax expenditures that also distort incentives include the lack of taxation of various non-wage employee benefits. The distortions introduced by the non-inclusion of private health-insurance premiums in workers' income are discussed in more detail in Chapter V; the direct cost to the Treasury is about $40 billion per year. Tax advantages for private pensions encourage saving, which is perhaps a valuable goal, but they cost the Treasury $50 billion per year in lost revenue. Thus, they would need to add more than $50 billion in private saving that would otherwise not occur in order to justify their current cost to national saving in the form of reduced tax revenue.

The measures discussed in the preceding paragraphs are more than sufficient to balance the budget. Indeed, just the first six items in the adjoining box would result in deficit reduction of 3.4 per cent of GDP, more than the estimated structural gap of 3 per cent of GDP, and this is before considering such proposals as a VAT, large-scale energy taxes or changes to income-tax rates. Note that all of these proposals are within the experience of other OECD countries: most have VATs, government cost-controls on health spending, and some tax imputed rents from owner-occupied housing, for example. Solutions to the U.S. budget situation are readily found; what is required is the will to implement them.

IV. The structural reform agenda: banking and trade

Over the past year or so, progress in structural reform has been unremarkable. A banking reform law was passed in 1991, after a more sweeping proposal by the Administration had been voted down in Congress. Its effect is to tighten substantially bank supervision and regulation. On trade policy, the United States reached an agreement for a North American Free Trade Area with Canada and Mexico, but the multilateral General Agreement on Tariff and Trade talks languished. While voluntary restraints on steel imports were allowed to expire, other quantitative trade restrictions – notably in the areas of textiles, certain agricultural products, automobiles and semiconductors – remained in place.

Banking reform

Early in 1991, the Administration proposed a comprehensive banking reform. The proposal was discussed in detail in last year's *Survey*. A bill was passed in December that was much more limited in many important respects than the original proposal. The bill shored up the Federal Deposit Insurance Corporation with additional capital and required regulators to restrict the activities of banks as their capital fell below certain levels. While these were important changes, Congress missed the opportunity to make further changes that would have improved the efficiency of U.S. financial system. In particular, the final bill failed to include proposals to remove remaining restrictions on interstate banking and to liberalise the rules on financial-service activities that banking organisations can undertake and on who can own a bank. While further action is unlikely in 1992, finishing the job begun in 1991 would leave the United States with a more efficient banking and financial system.

The 1991 banking reform law

The main regulatory change included in the Federal Deposit Insurance Corporation Improvement Act (FDICIA) of 1991 was to require "early intervention" by bank regulators. The intention of the proposal is to limit losses to the FDIC by requiring bank regulators to intervene when a bank's capital falls below certain levels. Banks (which for the rest of this section will denote most types of depository institutions including savings and loans) are to be divided into five categories based on various measures of their capital relative to assets. Those in the first two meet international requirements. Sanctions begin to be imposed when a bank misses one or more of the capital standards. These "undercapitalised" banks – the third group – are required to submit a plan to the FDIC (or other primary regulator) explaining how they intend to meet the capital standards. Only those in the top category will be allowed to pay interest rates more than 75 basis points above those prevailing in their local market, while undercapitalised banks will be prohibited from paying dividends and, in general, from expanding. "Significantly" undercapitalised banks face additional restrictions, and the primary regulator can, if it chooses, replace the management or other officers of such a bank or force its sale. Finally, the days of "critically" undercapitalised banks – with less than 2 per cent equity capital – are numbered. The primary regulator must shut down or force the sale of such institutions within 90 days unless it can explain why not doing so will save money for the relevant fund [either the Bank Insurance Fund (BIF) or the Savings Association Insurance Fund (SAIF)]. While capital is to provide the main indicator under early intervention, regulators will also have the authority to downgrade banks by one category for other reasons, such as perceived riskiness of operations, but may not use this power to downgrade a bank to the "critically undercapitalised" category.

Early intervention should help prevent one of the main problems that led to the savings and loan crisis: financial institutions operating with little or no shareholder capital at risk. When an institution with access to government deposit insurance is allowed to operate without adequate capital, there is a strong incentive to invest in very risky projects, even when the chance of a pay-off is slim: since they have already lost their investment, the shareholders can only gain from risky investments, even if there is only a small chance of a high return. Such an institution can attract deposits only because of the government's guarantee, and it is the taxpayer who is exposed to the high probability of the venture's failure. On the other hand, with a large amount of capital at stake, the owners of the bank stand to lose more before the government insurance fund has to pay out and so will have a larger incentive to monitor the bank's activities. The hope implicit in the FDICIA is that the restrictions on bank activities for low-capital institutions will limit future drains on the deposit-insurance system.

The FDICIA also provided for a $30 billion credit line from the Treasury to the FDIC to cover expected losses of troubled banks. This advance is to be eventually recovered through higher deposit-insurance premiums on banks. The bill also allowed for working-capital loans from the Treasury to the FDIC of up to 90 per cent of the "fair market value" of assets acquired from failed banks. It is estimated that this could amount to another $40 billion in credit extensions. Ample funds are important, because delays lead to added costs, mostly because of the moral-hazard problem just described: bankrupt banks have strong incentives to make risky loans that can eventually add to the cost of protecting insured depositors.

The bill also moved to restrict the ability of the FDIC to cover uninsured depositors in the event of a bank failure. In recent years, over 99 per cent of uninsured deposits were paid off, mainly because most failed banks were "resolved" via mergers (so-called purchase-and-assumption arrangements) rather than by liquidation. There was concern that implicitly extending deposit insurance in this way was adding to the taxpayer cost of insurance directly, and also indirectly by limiting the incentive for large depositors to keep tabs on the operations of their bank. The main change in the legislation was to require the FDIC to justify in each case the use of a purchase-and-assumption transaction, demonstrating that it was indeed cheaper, directly to the government, than liquidating the bank. The bill also moved to limit severely the ability of regulators to use the excuse that a bank was "too big to fail" as an exemption to the least-cost rule. Under the FDICIA, the too-big-to-fail exemption can be invoked only if there is perceived to be a risk of widespread disruptions to the banking or payments system (perhaps because of a triggering of runs on other banks). Approval of an exemption must be granted by the Secretary of the Treasury (in consultation with the President), two-thirds of the Federal Reserve Board and two-thirds of the FDIC Board of Directors. In a related move, the bill also restricted the Fed's ability to lend to critically undercapitalised banks, in an effort to limit the ability of uninsured depositors to withdraw their money.

A final important aspect of the FDICIA was to require the FDIC to adopt risk-based deposit insurance premiums by January 1994.[22] Relating deposit insurance premiums to risk could help make the deposit insurance system more economically efficient in several ways. First, it limits the implicit subsidy from safe banks to risky ones when all banks are charged the same insurance premium. Also, appropriate risk-basing would contribute to the incentives for banks to avoid excessively risky assets. As with any insurer, it will be difficult to assess risks of different activities. Some measures that can be used include the bank's overall capital level, its mix of assets and lending activities, and its maturity balance between assets and deposits.

The need for further reform

While the United States generally has one of the more liberal regulatory regimes among OECD countries, the banking sector is a marked exception. The Administration's 1991 reform proposal would have loosened the two most egregious restrictions: prohibitions on interstate branch banking and restrictions on bank ownership. Restrictions on interstate banking are particularly anachronistic. Although regulators, within the latitude provided by statutes, have managed to skirt much of the law limiting interstate banking and provisions for at least regional linkups exist in almost all states, remaining laws still raise the costs of truly national banking. Regional concentration of banks contributes to their instability, as illustrated by the problems first in farm lending in the early 1980s, Texas banks in the middle of the decade and New England banks by its end. Full interstate banking and branching would allow greater diversification of lending risks. It might also lead to some reduction in costs as banks merge, although the continuing existence of small banks alongside large ones in many markets suggest that the economies of scale in banking are not the only factor determining a competitive success.[23]

Last year's Administration proposal would have reformed the Depression-era laws that limit the affiliations between banks and other financial and non-financial institutions. These laws impose costs on the U.S. financial system and leave it out of step with practice in many other OECD countries. Restrictions that isolate commercial banks (which take deposits and make business loans) from investment banks and other financial institutions mean, for example, that banks cannot deal in corporate securities, adding considerable nuisance costs to retail banking clients. And on the lending side, the barriers between bank and non-bank financial firms can lead to unnecessary duplication of effort, since a client firm that needs both kinds of financial services must create a relationship with both. Restrictions on bank activities and affiliations are much less strict in most other major OECD countries. Hence, higher costs of intermediation in the United States are a disadvantage for U.S. non-financial firms in international competition.

One concern about linkages between banks and other firms is that they could lead to an implicit extension of the Federal banking "safety net", such as deposit insurance, discount window borrowing and payments-system guarantees, to other types of firms through bank ownership. Last year's Administration proposal included legal "firewalls" that were aimed at limiting such exposure. Also, the Administration would have limited link-ups to only the strongest banks, which would have further limited risks. Such precautions would be unnecessary if the safety net were unsubsidised and if banks were adequately supervised, problems that were the aim of last year's reform package. However, to the extent that such reforms will inevitably be imperfect, controls on banking linkages are probably justified.[24]

The United States on the world trade scene

Domestic market protection

As both the world's largest economy and the largest trader, the United States has a strong interest and an important role in fostering the health of the international trading system. It has led the way in the past 40 years toward greater freedom through the series of multilateral tariff reductions negotiated through the General Agreement on Tariffs and Trade (GATT) and has maintained relatively open markets. Indeed, its average tariff is fairly low (a weighted average of only 5.1 per cent according to the GATT), and imports of both goods and services have trended up as a share of GDP over the past 30 years, in contrast to relatively stagnant trade shares for both the EC and Japan.

Over the past decade in the United States, as in many other OECD countries, there has been an increase in pressures for protectionism. U.S. recourse to unilateral actions in its international commercial relations, often claimed to be directed toward achieving fair trade, has been a matter of concern. The strength of the dollar in the first half of the 1980s was probably the main underlying factor behind poor trade performance, but protectionist pressures have persisted – albeit possibly abated in degree – despite the subsequent exchange-rate depreciation and the ensuing substantial reduction in the external deficit. To a large extent, successive administrations have managed to resist these pressures. However, non-tariff measures increasingly substituted for tariff protection in the 1980s, so that in recent years, for example, nearly 30 per cent of Japan's and 34 per cent of Mexican exports to the United States have been restricted in some fashion. Voluntary restraint arrangements (VRAs) are prominent as a means of restricting imports in certain sectors, covering nearly 9 per cent of total imports in 1990, down from a peak of nearly 11 per cent in 1986.[25] Besides their obvious trade-restraining impact, VRAs encourage anti-competitive actions by foreign firms which could, were it not for official compulsion, be prosecuted under U.S. antitrust laws. Most recently, machine-tool VRAs with Japan and Taiwan were extended, upon their expiry at end-1991, but are to be progressively phased out by end-1993.

The GATT permits countervailing and anti-dumping duties as remedies against injurious trade practices; however, the proceedings involved impose a heavy burden on defendant firms, and they may be sometimes used to prevent foreign firms from competing aggressively in the domestic market. While countervailing duties investigations have waned in importance in the United States, anti-dumping cases remain numerous: most recently, for example, twelve U.S. steel producers requested anti-dumping and/or countervailing investigation, after VRAs expired in March 1992 and negotiations on a multilateral steel agreement broke down. At end-1990, 71 countervailing measures and 195 anti-dumping measures were in place, many of which had been introduced decades earlier. The concern of trading partners has also been raised by:

- tariff reclassifications which result in higher duties; the prime example is that of two-door utility vehicles which, for the past several years, have been classified as trucks (attracting a 25 per cent duty), rather than cars (dutiable at only 2½ per cent), contradicting international norms;
- the extension in April 1992 by the U.S. Justice Department of the existing extraterritorial application of U.S. antitrust laws to include

foreign cartels hindering U.S. exports even if no harm is done to U.S. consumers;

– Buy America restrictions, which give domestic producers a price advantage of at least 6 per cent in certain categories of government procurement. However, the United States has stated its willingness to negotiate reciprocal removals of these restrictions with other countries.

To some extent domestic-market protection has been increased and exports to the United States have been reduced from levels which would have otherwise prevailed by the imposition of a variety of fees, penalties and regulations. An *ad valorem* fee on customs, harbour and other arrival facilities, was instituted in 1986, although it was modified in 1990 after it was found not to be in conformity with GATT provisions. Corporate Average Fuel Economy (CAFE) requirements and penalties – because they allow fuel economy to be determined as an average of each firm's different models – indirectly discriminate against some automobile producers from Europe, who lack the product range over which to average fuel-economy performance of their more expensive models. On the other hand, Japanese producers benefited from CAFE standards. CAFE standards, along with

Table 16. **Anti-dumping and countervailing duty actions by the United States**

Period (year ending in June)	Anti-dumping		Countervailing duties		
	Investigations	Definitive duties	Investigations	Provisional measures	Definitive duties
1981	13	4	7	5	3
1982	25	3	75	46	9
1983	38	7	35	34	23
1984	44	22	22	17	11
1985	61	13	60	39	21
1986	65	25	43	24	17
1987	40	30	11	16	16
1988	33	22	13	9	10
1989	62	27	16	9	11
1990	27	17	6	4	4
1991[1]	57	19	5	1	2
Total	465	189	293	204	127

1. Only through May.
Source: GATT Secretariat.

73

the luxury excise tax and the "gas guzzler" tax, have raised $558 million since their inception, of which fully 88 per cent has been paid by European producers, compared with their 4 per cent market share. Finally, in the United States as in other OECD countries access to the domestic market has been restricted by the imposition of a multiplicity of standards, and sanitary or environmental regulations, although these are imposed uniformly on U.S. and foreign producers. Kiwi fruit, tuna and wine are examples of products subject to recent changes in regulations, but the ongoing costs to many foreign traders are severe given the 2700 different state and local governments which require safety certifications for products sold or installed in their jurisdiction.

The agriculture sector has been especially protected in OECD countries, with transfers from consumers and governments to producers reaching over $300 billion in recent years. The United States is responsible for over one-sixth of this total, although the level of U.S. agricultural protection as measured by the

Table 17. **Trends in agricultural protection**

	1979-86 Average	1987	1988	1989	1990[1]	1991[2]	1992[3]
United States							
Net total producer subsidy equivalent ($ billion)	30.6	44.2	36.9	32.2	35.3	34.7	n.a.
Net percentage producer subsidy equivalent	28	40	34	28	29	30	30
Net total consumer subsidy equivalent ($ billion)	−16.6	−21.1	−17.6	−16.3	−20.3	−19.6	n.a.
Percentage consumer subsidy equivalent	−18	−23	−18	−16	−19	−19	−18
OECD							
Net total producer subsidy equivalent ($ billion)	107.2	174.3	166.0	147.9	180.2	177.0	n.a.
Net percentage producer subsidy equivalent	37	49	45	40	45	45	44
Net total consumer subsidy equivalent ($ billion)	−74.2	−135.0	−129.7	−111.4	−133.0	−134.7	n.a.
Percentage consumer subsidy equivalent	−28	−41	−37	−32	−36	−37	−36

1. Estimated.
2. Provisional.
3. Projected.
Source: OECD estimates.

percentage "producer subsidy equivalent" (PSE) is only two-thirds the OECD average. While some significant progress was made in reducing protection in the late 1980s, progress has stalled since then in the United States as well as elsewhere in the OECD. On balance, the 1990 Farm Act did not represent a move toward market orientation, although it did increase planting flexibility under farm support programmes. In 1991, total PSE was $35 billion, as in 1990: a decrease in production volume offset an increase in percentage PSE. VRAs were negotiated – the first since 1988 – on beef and veal from Australia and New Zealand in order to avoid the imposition of quotas under the 1979 Meat Import Act. And, reversing the easing of the past several years, the sugar import quota was cut by 34 per cent, despite its cost to consumers ($1.1 billion in 1989).

Market access abroad

The U.S. has also moved to facilitate the access of its exporters to foreign markets. Recourse to some unilateral actions to achieve this goal has raised concerns among trading partners. Section 301 of the 1974 Trade Act allows U.S. trade-policy makers to threaten trade retaliation if others' unfair trade practices are not removed. Such "aggressive unilateralism" has caused frictions (the United States alone determining what constitutes an unfair practice and others being required to liberalise unilaterally), especially since the 1988 Omnibus Trade and Competitiveness Act obliged the President to use "Super 301" to improve access to foreign markets. "Super 301", which expired at the end of 1990, required the U.S. Trade Representative to identify priority countries exhibiting a pattern of unfair trade barriers and to undertake investigations and seek negotiations with a view to their elimination. Japan, Brazil and India were so designated in 1989 and by end-1990, when such authority lapsed, agreements had been reached with all but India. Also, "Special 301", instituted in the 1988 Act, brought the protection of intellectual property rights into this domain for the first time. In 1991, China, India and Thailand were designated under "Special 301", but China has since avoided retaliation by signing a bilateral agreement. The U.S. Administration opposes legislation to reinstate "Super 301" authority.

The impact of the trade-policy stance embodied in Section 301 has been hotly debated. From a narrow vantage point of leading to improved market access for U.S. exporters it has apparently been at least partially successful in over half of all cases (Bayard and Elliott, 1992), especially for those involving traditional

Table 18. Number of Section 301 cases

Number of cases involving explicit threats or retaliation in parentheses

Product or practice	1975-79				1980-84				1985-89				1990-91				1975-91			
	EC	Japan	Other	Total	EC	Japan	Other	Total	EC	Japan	Other	Total	EC	Japan	Other	Total	EC	Japan	Other	Total
Manufacturing	½	2½ (1)	2	5 (1)	1	1 (1)	8 (1)	10 (2)	1	4 (4)	4 (3)	9 (7)			1	1	2½	7½ (6)	15 (4)	25 (10)
Agriculture	8 (2)	2	1	11 (2)	4 (2)		4	8 (2)	5 (4)	2 (1)	8 (4)	15 (9)	2 (1)			2 (1)	19 (9)	4 (1)	13 (4)	36 (14)
Services			5 (3)	5 (3)	1		2 (1)	3 (1)		1 (1)	2 (2)	3 (3)					1	1 (1)	9 (6)	11 (7)
Intellectual property rights											4 (4)	4 (4)			4	4			8 (8)	8 (8)
Total cases	8½ (2)	4½ (1)	8 (3)	21 (6)	6 (2)	1 (1)	14 (2)	21 (5)	6 (4)	7 (6)	18 (13)	31 (23)	2 (1)		5 (4)	7 (5)	22½ (9)	12½ (8)	45 (22)	80 (39)

Source: Bayard and Elliott (1992).

76

trade barriers against which there was an explicit threat of retaliation and those which were self-initiated. Explicit threats have been resorted to much more frequently since 1985; accordingly, there has been a rising "success rate". However, in some cases success has been only nominal, with another form of protection substituting for the irritant, and retaliations undertaken when no successful outcome could be negotiated were often ineffective. In any case, the efficacy of 301 relative to the more traditional means of opening foreign markets through the GATT's multilateral mechanisms is unclear, although GATT does not currently have the means to negotiate the reduction of many of the types of protectionist policies to which Section 301 investigations are addressed. Nevertheless, the risk of triggering a trade war should not be underestimated.

The Uruguay Round

The United States has been a strong advocate of the trade liberalisation aimed at under the GATT's Uruguay Round. After nearly six years, the negotiations are, at the time of writing, approaching a definitive stage. While some sort of agreement may be patched together, time is running out for negotiators to come to an agreement which can be submitted to Congress before the "fast-track" authority expires.[26] In late 1991 GATT Director General Arthur Dunkel proposed a draft compromise agreement based on the negotiations to that point.[27] The agricultural negotiations are the major stumbling block; if an agreement in this sector can be reached between the United States and the European Community, it will be possible to proceed multilaterally with the negotiation of specific concessions to be offered by individual countries.

Progress since the Dunkel text was proposed has been limited. While the recently agreed reform of the EC's Common Agricultural Policy (CAP) is a step on its part, U.S. negotiators note that the recent CAP reform did not address export subsidies and market access nor product-specific problems such as oil-seeds, sugar, fruit and vegetables. Since no GATT agreement was reached as of end-June 1992, the Omnibus Budget Reconciliation Act of 1990 requires the Administration to increase agricultural export subsidies by $1 billion per year in fiscal years 1994 and 1995. Separately, in the summer of 1992 the Administration announced its intention to increase U.S. farm export subsidies by up to $1 billion during the next year under the Export Enhancement Program. Additionally, a number of trade disputes, especially the oilseeds case, have been held in abeyance pending the outcome of the Round.[28]

Besides agriculture, one of the areas for which most hope was held out for progress in this Round was textiles. Like agriculture, this sector has been excluded from the usual GATT disciplines; textiles trade has been governed by the Multi-Fibre Arrangement (MFA).[29] According to U.S. International Trade Commission estimates, the MFA cost U.S. consumers $10.7 billion in 1988 and reduced welfare by $2.5 billion that same year. Under the draft Dunkel text, the MFA would be phased out over a ten-year transition period. Other features of the working text would limit trade-policy measures (notably the elimination of "grey-area measures" such as VRAs, a clarification of antidumping rules and procedures and reform of GATT's dispute settlement mechanism), but others provide the United States with much of what it has sought from the Uruguay Round (the establishment of a General Agreement on Trade in Services, explicit prohibition of "trade-related investment measures" and new rules governing intellectual property rights). In addition, an eventual agreement would probably include a substantial tariff reduction, perhaps on the order of one-third.

Progress toward a North American Free Trade Area

The United States supports the "most-favoured-nation" principle underlying the GATT, while continuing to seek out regional free trade agreements which are explicitly permitted under the GATT. After the U.S.-Canada accord came into effect in 1989, the Administration turned its attention to Mexico, and negotiations began with that country and Canada toward the formation of a North American Free Trade Area (NAFTA)[30] in June 1991. Negotiations were concluded in the summer of 1992, and the agreement is subject to the 1993 "fast-track" deadlines for Congressional approval. NAFTA would achieve tariff elimination, as much reduction as possible in non-tariff barriers, national (non-discriminatory) treatment for a wide range of services producers and foreign investors and better protection for intellectual property rights. The arrangement will promote economic growth and the efficient use of human and natural resources in North America. Model simulations suggest that under NAFTA the United States would stand to gain about 1/2 per cent in output from static scale-economy and intra-industry specialisation effects alone in the long run. In addition to static gains from trade, increased investment opportunities and the support offered by

NAFTA for Mexico's stabilisation programme should lead to faster growth as well. Trade would expand, but there would probably be little impact on the balance of trade with the rest of the world. Most studies project modest increases in U.S. employment and average wages.[31] The principal sectors to benefit in the United States would be grain farming and financial institutions, along with a variety of manufacturing sectors such as transportation equipment. U.S. imports of crude and refined petroleum and products, fresh and processed fruit and vegetables and textiles and apparel stand to rise as well.

A number of fears have been expressed regarding the NAFTA. The most important from the vantage point of U.S. domestic interests are the low-wage competition from Mexico and inadequate Mexican enforcement of labour and environmental standards. But it is clear that highly developed economies like that of the United States will have less and less scope for the production of unskilled-labour-intensive goods and services whether or not there is a NAFTA. The appropriate response must be an improvement in the average skill levels of the least educated American workers with a focus on those most directly affected. The United States' other trading partners in Europe and Asia are apprehensive that their exporters will be squeezed out of North American markets through trade diversion effects and that realisation of the NAFTA could diminish the U.S. commitment to the GATT. However, the processes of completing the Round and the NAFTA are complementary due to the similarity of problems to be overcome in textiles and agriculture for example. Accordingly, the benefits which may accrue to the rest of the world from the Agreement are likely to depend on the success of the Round. Finally, the other party to the negotiations, Canada, fears a reduction of its advantages in the U.S. market, especially as the U.S. Administration has signalled its intention to negotiate future trade agreements in order to form an eventual hemispheric free trade zone under the 1990 Enterprise for the Americas Initiative.[32]

Looking beyond the upcoming crucial period regarding the Uruguay Round and the NAFTA, it is to be hoped that international trade tensions will ease. The United States, along with other OECD countries, can make an effective contribution to that end by agreeing to strengthen multilateral dispute settlement procedures and to comply with GATT panel recommendations. Furthermore, bilateralism in its dealings with certain trading partners, especially Japan, has probably gone too far and risks excessive management of trade. For example, the U.S.-

Japan semiconductor agreement of August 1991 specifies, as one indicator of market access, an expected foreign market share in Japan of 20 per cent by end-1992. Result-based criteria of this sort could potentially lead to trade patterns that do not reflect comparative advantage. Furthermore, if the expectation is not realised, it could create difficulties for the bilateral relationship. Another example of managed trade is the January 1992 agreement on auto parts. Japanese producers in the United States are expected to increase their share of parts procured locally from 50 to 70 per cent, while local parts procurement and U.S. parts exports to Japan would rise substantially, reaching $19 billion in 1994. Such cartelisation of trade may lead to a reduction of competitive pressures on costs and prices as well as on innovation.

V.   Health-care reform

Introduction

Health-care reform has moved to the top of the policy agenda in the United States, as the high and rising costs of financing the system have intensified a long-standing debate about the affordability of, and access to, health care. While the intensity of U.S. health care – as measured by physician education, staffing per hospital bed, and other standards – rose substantially in the 1980s, an increasingly broad spectrum of the population has begun to worry about health-care finances. Many individuals are facing rapidly rising health-care insurance premiums and out-of-pocket expenses. There are also indications that insurers are less willing to cover bad health risks than before, as mounting costs force them to seek new ways of economising. Employers, who provide the bulk of health-care insurance for the non-aged, are increasingly worried about the soaring cost of premiums. Federal and state governments, which run two large public pro- grammes – Medicare (purely Federal) for those over 65 years of age and Medi- caid (joint state-Federal) for some of the poor – are concerned about the growing strain on their finances. These developments affect those most in need of insur- ance; that is, those at risk of having, or those who already have, chronic and expensive illnesses. Against this general background the heightened fear of unemployment in the recent recession and its aftermath has also played a role in raising the profile of health care, as the heavy reliance on employer-provided group insurance plans means that losing, or even changing, a job can result in losing health-insurance cover.

The U.S. health-care financing system has two characteristics that define the current policy concerns: high and rising costs and a substantial number of people without adequate health-care insurance. These characteristics also distinguish the United States from other OECD countries. Far more is spent on health care in the

United States than elsewhere: per capita health expenditures are almost twice the OECD average. Moreover, as a share of GDP, these expenditures are increasing rapidly in the United States, while they have stabilised, or at least slowed, in most other OECD countries during the last decade. These trends reflect the largely unconstrained, high and growing U.S. demand for quality health care. Judging by indicators such as infant mortality and life expectancy, the larger outlays have not resulted in better health. However, it is widely recognised that such indicators are far too crude to be useful in judging the effectiveness of health care, and those Americans who have insurance coverage may be getting more for their outsized expenditures than they would suggest.[33] In fact, most Americans are fairly satisfied with their health care. On the other hand, there are some 35 million Americans who do not have any insurance coverage, and most of them receive relatively inadequate medical care and often at a rather late stage in their sickness. The share of Americans without health coverage has risen slightly in the past decade; most of them are young adults and are uninsured for relatively short periods of time. However, and in contrast, coverage in other OECD countries is essentially complete. The extension of coverage and cost containment without reducing the quality of health-care delivery are now seen as the two key issues facing U.S. health-care policy, although increasing access raises demand for medical services, thereby putting additional pressure on expenditures.

This chapter first documents the nature and sources of the increases in health-care expenses in the United States, both over time and relative to other OECD countries. The issue of access to health care – the gaps in insurance coverage – is then taken up. The third section lays out policy alternatives for containing costs and increasing access. An Annex describes the health-care financing systems of the United States and of the other larger OECD countries, except Italy (which is discussed extensively in the forthcoming OECD Economic Survey of Italy).

The rising cost of health care

Trends in health-care expenditures

Total health-care spending in the United States grew at an annualised rate of nearly 6 per cent from 1960 to 1990, after adjustment for changes in the overall

Table 19. **Growth in total health-care expenditure**

1987 constant dollars, billions [1]

Average annual percentage change

	1970-1990	1960-1965	1965-1970	1970-1975	1975-1980	1980-1985	1985-1990
Total	5.5	7.3	7.4	4.9	5.4	5.7	6.1
Private	5.1	7.2	3.6	3.5	5.2	5.9	5.7
Public	6.2	7.4	16.6	7.2	5.7	5.3	6.6
Federal	6.6	8.9	24.2	7.9	6.5	6.0	6.1
State and local	5.4	6.6	7.6	6.1	4.2	3.8	7.7

1. Nominal expenditures divided by the GDP deflator.
Source: OECD.

price level, as measured by the GDP deflator. The growth rate during the 1960s was rather higher, just over 7¼ per cent, largely because the introduction of Medicare and Medicaid in 1965 greatly expanded the access to, and the demand for, medical care. As there have been no institutional changes of similar nature and importance since, the evolution of the current system of health-care delivery and financing can best be analysed by considering the 1970 to 1990 period, during which health spending grew at an annual rate of 5½ per cent in excess of

Table 20. **Components of total health-care expenditure**

	1960	1965	1970	1975	1980	1985	1990
	As a percentage of total health-care expenditure						
Private	75.5	75.3	62.8	58.5	57.8	58.3	57.6
Public	24.5	24.7	37.2	41.5	42.2	41.7	42.0
Federal	10.7	11.6	23.9	27.4	28.9	29.4	28.7
State and local	13.8	13.2	13.3	14.1	13.3	12.2	13.3
	As a percentage of GDP						
Total	**5.3**	**5.9**	**7.4**	**8.4**	**9.3**	**10.7**	**12.4**
Private	4.0	4.5	4.6	4.9	5.4	6.3	7.1
Public	1.3	1.5	2.7	3.5	3.9	4.4	5.2
Federal	0.6	0.7	1.8	2.3	2.7	3.1	3.5
State and local	0.7	0.8	1.0	1.2	1.2	1.3	1.6

Source: Congressional Research Service (1991); Levit *et al.* (1991); OECD.

inflation – twice as fast as real GDP. As a result, the share of GDP devoted to health-care spending rose from 7.4 per cent in 1970 to 12.1 per cent in 1990. The share of GDP absorbed by health-care spending will rise to almost 16½ per cent by the year 2000 (Sonnefeld *et al.*, 1991) if present cost trends continue. With a rapidly ageing population in the early part of the next century, health spending could reach 25 per cent by 2030 (Warshawsky, 1991*a*).

The increases in outlays have been fairly widespread across expenditure categories, leaving their shares of total health spending roughly unchanged. Since 1970, the share of hospital care in total health spending rose only slightly, with an increase during the 1970s being mostly reversed in the 1980s as cost-containment measures were introduced in the Medicare and Medicaid programmes. The share of outlays for physician services has also been roughly constant since 1970, at 17 to 19 per cent of the total, although it began to rise steeply at the end of the 1980s. Outlay increases in excess of the rise in overall medical expenditures occurred during the 1970s in nursing homes, whose share in overall expenditures rose from 6½ to 8 per cent, largely owing to coverage under Medicaid. By contrast, the share of drugs and other non-durables fell substantially, from almost 12 per cent of the total in 1970 to about 8 per cent in 1980. Since then, outlays on drugs have grown at about the same rate as most other medical expenditures.

Table 21. **Health-care spending by category**

Percentage of total health-care expenditures

	1960	1965	1970	1975	1980	1985	1990
Personal	88.1	85.6	87.3	87.7	87.7	87.5	87.9
Hospital care	34.2	33.7	37.6	39.4	40.9	39.8	38.4
Nursing home care	3.6	4.1	6.5	7.5	8.0	8.1	8.0
Physicians	19.5	19.7	18.3	17.5	16.7	17.5	18.9
Dentists	7.2	6.7	6.3	6.2	5.7	5.5	5.1
Drugs[1]	15.7	14.2	11.8	9.8	8.6	8.6	8.2
Medical durables [2]	3.0	3.0	2.7	2.3	1.8	1.7	1.8
Other	4.9	4.2	4.1	5.0	5.8	6.4	7.5
Non-personal[3]	11.9	14.4	12.7	12.3	12.3	12.5	12.1

1. Includes medical non-durables.
2. Includes "vision products".
3. Includes construction, non-commercial research, government public health activities, programme administration and the net cost of private health insurance.
Source: OECD.

Increases in real health-care expenditures reflect both the relative price of health care – the amount by which the prices of health-care services have risen in excess of the prices of other goods – and the quantity of services delivered. The Health Care Financing Administration (HCFA) has developed deflators for personal health care[34] by constructing input-cost measures for some components (hospitals and nursing homes) and using consumer price index data for others (physician services, for example). The deflators do not take changes in the quality of new medical procedures fully into account, and therefore may overstate price increases.[35]

Of the average annual increase in real expenditure on total health care (deflated by the GDP deflator) of just over 5½ per cent from 1970 to 1990, about

Table 22. **Growth in price and volume of total health-care expenditures**

Average annual growth rates

	1960-1965	1965-1970	1970-1975	1975-1980	1980-1985	1985-1990[1]	1970-1990[1]
Real expenditure[2]							
Total	7.3	7.4	4.9	5.4	5.7	6.1	5.5
Hospitals and nursing homes	7.3	10.8	6.2	6.3	5.2	5.4	5.8
Physicians	7.5	5.8	4.0	4.5	6.6	7.7	5.7
Relative prices[3]							
Total	0.7	1.0	−0.2	1.1	2.6	2.7	1.5
Hospitals and nursing homes	1.5	1.9	0.6	1.3	2.3	2.0	1.5
Physicians	1.2	1.9	−0.1	1.9	2.9	3.9	2.1
Volume[4]							
Total	6.5	6.4	5.2	4.2	3.1	3.2	3.9
Hospitals and nursing homes	5.7	8.7	5.6	5.0	2.9	3.3	4.2
Physicians	6.2	3.8	4.2	2.5	3.6	3.7	3.5
Volume per capita							
Total	4.4	5.7	4.3	3.3	2.0	2.3	3.0
Hospitals and nursing homes	4.2	7.6	4.7	4.0	1.9	2.3	3.2
Physicians	4.7	2.7	3.3	1.6	2.6	2.6	2.5
Memorandum							
Real GDP	4.8	2.8	2.2	3.2	2.9	3.0	2.8
Real per capita GDP	3.4	1.8	1.3	2.3	1.9	2.0	1.9
GDP deflator	1.5	4.6	7.0	7.7	5.1	3.3	5.8

1. Data for 1990 are preliminary.
2. Nominal health-care expenditures divided by the GDP deflator.
3. Medical price deflators for personal health care divided by the GDP deflator.
4. Nominal expenditure divided by medical price deflators for personal health care.
Source: OECD.

1½ percentage points is attributable to increases in the relative price of medical care – that is, to the increase in health-care costs in excess of general inflation.[36] The rest represents volume increases, of which about 1 percentage point reflects population growth. Thus, the per capita volume of medical services has grown at 3 per cent per year, significantly above real GDP per capita (1.9 per cent), indicating a real-income elasticity of about 1.6. These long-term averages mask an acceleration of real spending and a shift from volume to relative price growth that occurred in the 1980s: the average increase in relative prices moved up from 0.4 per cent per year in the 1970s to 2.6 per cent in the 1980s. Increases in the consumer price index for prescription drugs, for example, have far exceeded overall inflation over the past decade. Growth in deflated expenditures picked up in the 1980s, reaching more than 6 per cent by the end of the decade, despite the fact that volume growth tailed off, especially for hospitals and drugs.

Diagram 14. **RELATIVE INFLATION RATE OF PRESCRIPTION DRUGS**
12 month percentage change[1]

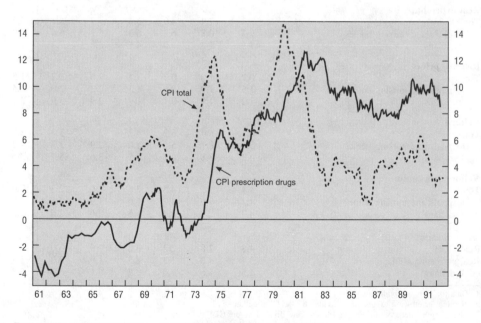

1. Four-quarter percentage change prior to 1970 for prescription-drug prices.
Source: Bureau of Labor Statistics.

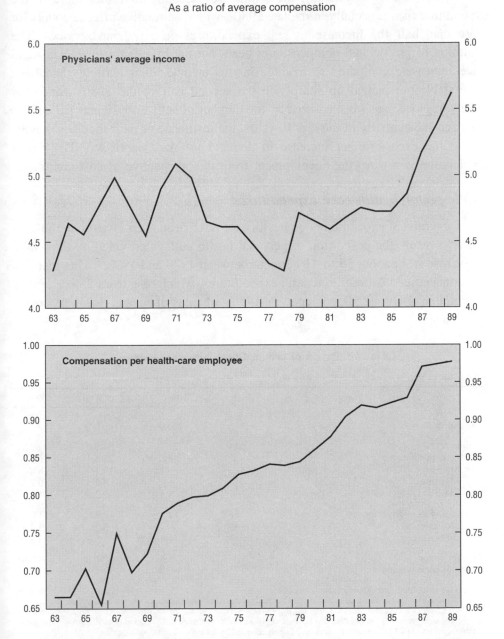

Diagram 15. **COMPENSATION OF HEALTH-CARE PROVIDERS**
As a ratio of average compensation

Physicians' average income

Compensation per health-care employee

Source: OECD.

In the case of physicians, price increases account for rather more of the expenditure rise, especially in the late 1980s, when the relative price accounts for more than half the increase in real expenditures on physician services. The evolution of physicians' compensation bears out the impression of recent rapid price increases: compared to average labour income, their earnings had been quite stable but picked up sharply in the second half of the 1980s. Since the supply of physicians (as measured by the number of active physicians per capita) has risen substantially in the last 30 years, the resilience of their incomes may be due to the even stronger increase in demand for their services.[37] The recent acceleration is a worrying development from the perspective of cost control.

Public-sector health-care expenditures

Government expenditures on health care have risen even faster than the total and, as a result, the proportion of personal health outlays provided by the public sector rose from about 35 to 41 per cent between 1970 and 1990.[38] This increase was concentrated entirely in federal expenditures, which rose from 23 per cent of the total in 1970 to 30 per cent in 1990, whereas state and local payments

Table 23. **Payers of personal health-care expenditures**[1]

Per cent

	1960	1970	1990
Total expenditures	100.0	100.0	100.0
Public sector	21.4	34.5	41.3
Federal government	8.8	22.5	30.3
Medicare	–	11.1	18.6
Medicaid	–	4.2	6.9
Other	8.8	7.2	4.7
State and local governments	12.6	12.0	11.0
Medicaid	–	3.5	5.2
Other	12.6	8.5	5.8
Private sector	78.6	65.4	58.7
Out-of-pocket payments	55.9	39.4	23.3
Private insurance and other private sources	22.7	26.0	35.4

1. Personal health-care expenditures ($583.3 billion in 1990) differ from national health expenditures ($666.2 billion) in that they exclude programme administration and net cost of private health insurance ($38.7 billion in 1990), government public health activities ($19.3 billion) and research and construction ($22.8 billion).
Source: Levit *et al.* (1991).

maintained a share of 10 to 12 per cent, with no clear trend. The federal government bears a much larger share of government health-care outlays, paying for all of Medicare and a matching share of Medicaid. These outlays have grown faster than private costs: Medicare and Medicaid expenditures grew at 8 and 7½ per cent annual rates in real terms between 1970 and 1990. According to the projections of Sonnefeld *et al.* (1991), the state and local share will remain roughly stable for the rest of the decade, but the federal share will rise to 32 per cent.

The share of federal and state budgets devoted to health-care outlays has also risen rapidly: health-care expenditures rose from 8.5 per cent of total federal expenditures in 1970 to 15.3 per cent in 1990, and from 7.4 to 11.4 per cent of state expenditures. The pressure on government budgets has led some states to attempt to reduce Medicaid expenditures, although their ability to do so is

Diagram 16. **GOVERNMENT HEALTH-CARE EXPENDITURES**
As a percentage of total government expenditures

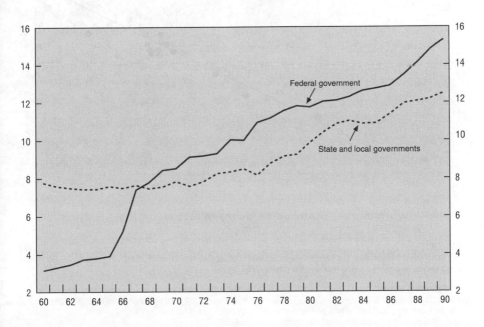

Source: Congressional Research Service (1991).

89

restricted by federal regulation. In its FY 1993 Budget, the Administration suggested capping expenditures on mandatory programmes, including Medicare, which could imply reductions in service if medical-care prices continue to rise more rapidly than the overall price level.

The full extent of Federal health-care expenditures is substantially understated by these figures, because they do not take into account the employer tax

Diagram 17. **HEALTH-CARE EXPENDITURES AND GDP: 1990**

$ 000s[1] per capita

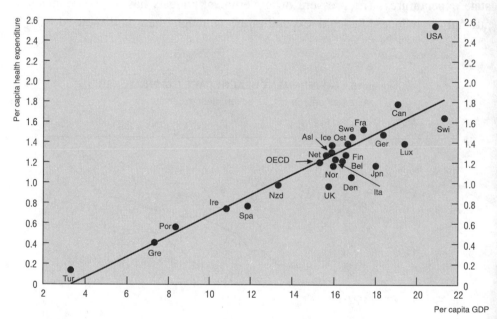

Note: The line represents a simple regression with the following results:
Per capita health spending = -.342 +.101 * Per capita GDP (1)
  (1.99)   (9.31)

$R^2 = 0.79$ SEE = 0.22
Omitting the United States from the sample yields an even better fit:
Per capita health spending = -.199 +.089 * Per capita GDP (2)
  (1.94)   (13.61)

$R^2 = 0.89$ SEE = 0.13
Based on (2) i.e. if the U.S. health system were typical of those in other OECD countries, health spending per capita would be reduced by $238 billion (4.4 per cent of GDP).
1. Using 1990 purchasing-power-parity exchange rates for GDP.
Source: OECD.

90

deduction of the health-insurance premiums that they pay on behalf of their employees.[39] These payments are not added to the taxable income of employees and therefore escape taxation altogether. The Congressional Research Service (1990*d*) estimates that the revenue lost as a result of this tax concession rose from $2.8 billion in 1970 to $29.6 billion in 1990, implying that the federal share of total health-care expenditures inclusive of this tax concession was nearly 4 percentage points higher in 1970, and 4¹/₂ percentage points higher in 1990, compared with the estimates cited above. The Office of Management and Budget (Budget of the United States Government, Fiscal Year 1993) estimates that the revenue lost rose to $36.2 billion in 1991. These figures are also underestimates, because the revenue lost from the concession is less than the so-called outlay equivalent, which is conceptually comparable to other government outlays.[40] The estimated outlay equivalent was $45.5 billion in 1991. To put these figures in perspective, in 1991 total federal outlays for Medicare (net of premiums collected) were $104.5 billion and federal Medicaid grants to states were $52.5 billion.

A Comparison with other OECD Countries

The rise in health-care expenditures in the United States has outstripped that of all other OECD countries by a wide margin, whether measured in per capita terms (adjusted for different rates of inflation in different countries) or, even more clearly, as a percent of GDP. The gap became particularly marked in the 1980s, when expenditures in some other countries decelerated while those in the United States picked up. It should be cautioned, however, that there is no single correct share of GDP spent on health care. National differences in shares may reflect different demands for health care, either in terms of its volume or its quality. The high and increasing demand for health care in the U.S. may reflect the needs of an increasingly affluent and aged population. When national supplies of health care are less than perfectly elastic, increases in the demand for health care may naturally raise the marginal cost of providing that additional care for some period of time.

Using price deflators similar to the HCFA deflators discussed above, it is possible to decompose the real growth into the relative price and volume of health care. While volume growth has been high in many countries, especially Japan and France, it has usually been in line with GDP growth, at least in the

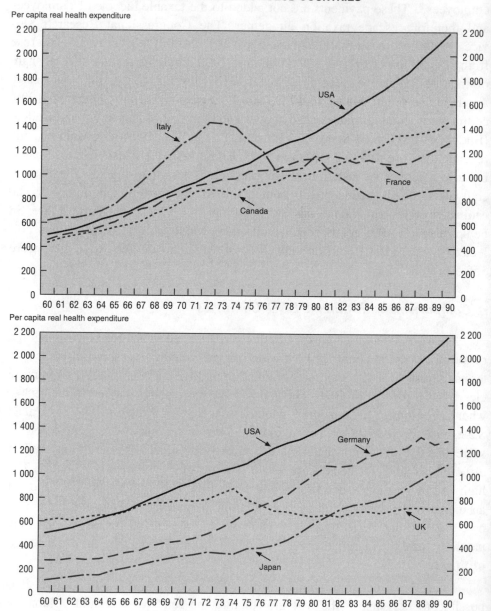

Diagram 18. **PER CAPITA HEALTH-CARE EXPENDITURES IN THE SEVEN LARGEST OECD COUNTRIES[1]**

1. Divided by GDP deflators and adjusted by purchasing power parities.
Source: OECD.

92

Diagram 19. **HEALTH-CARE EXPENDITURES OF THE SEVEN LARGEST OECD COUNTRIES**
as a percent of GDP

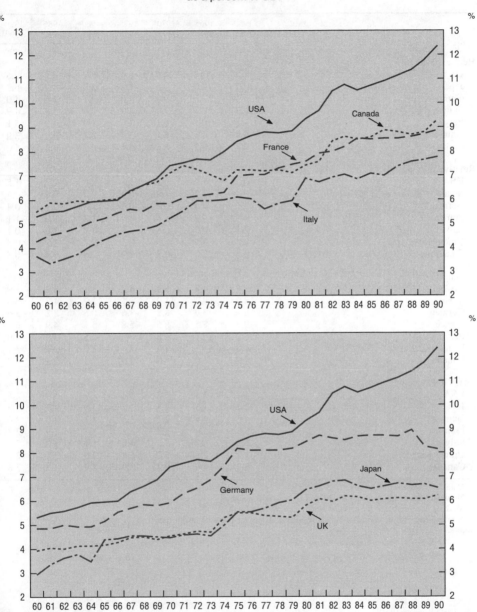

Source: OECD.

Table 24. **Health-care expenditures: an international comparison**

Average annual growth rates

	1960-1965	1965-1970	1970-1975	1975-1980	1980-1985	1985-1990[1]	1970-1990[1]
Real expenditure[2]							
USA	7.3	7.4	4.9	5.4	5.7	6.1	5.5
Japan	18.4	12.0	9.0	7.8	3.7	4.9	6.3
Germany	6.1	7.0	9.0	4.0	1.7	1.6	4.0
France	10.2	7.7	7.0	4.9	3.8	3.8	4.9
Italy	9.1	10.1	6.1	7.4	1.9	4.9	5.1
United Kingdom	4.4	4.3	6.1	2.9	2.7	3.9	3.9
Canada	7.7	8.2	5.6	4.4	5.9	4.2	5.0
Relative prices[3]							
USA	0.7	1.0	−0.2	1.1	2.6	2.7	1.5
Japan	0.4	2.2	−1.8	0.7	0.8	0.6	0.1
Germany	−0.2	3.0	0.7	0.4	1.2	−0.5	0.4
France	0.3	0.2	−1.4	−0.9	−1.2	−1.0	−1.1
Italy	2.1	0.0	−0.6	0.7	−0.7	1.0	0.1
United Kingdom	8.7	−9.5	−1.5	0.5	0.7	1.7	0.3
Canada	0.6	2.0	−0.8	0.7	2.6	0.9	0.8
Volume[4]							
USA	6.5	6.4	5.2	4.2	3.1	3.2	3.9
Japan	18.0	9.7	11.0	7.1	2.9	4.2	6.3
Germany	6.4	3.9	8.2	3.6	0.5	2.2	3.6
France	9.9	7.5	8.6	5.8	5.1	4.9	6.1
Italy	6.9	10.1	6.8	6.6	2.5	3.9	4.9
United Kingdom	−4.0	15.3	7.7	2.4	2.0	2.1	3.5
Canada	7.0	6.0	6.5	3.6	3.3	3.3	4.2
Real GDP							
USA	4.8	2.8	2.2	3.2	2.9	3.0	2.8
Japan	9.1	11.5	4.4	4.5	3.6	4.7	4.3
Germany	4.8	4.1	2.2	3.3	1.1	3.0	2.4
France	5.8	5.4	3.3	3.2	1.5	2.9	2.7
Italy	5.2	6.2	2.8	4.8	1.4	3.0	3.0
United Kingdom	3.2	2.5	2.0	1.8	2.0	3.1	2.2
Canada	5.7	4.6	5.2	3.9	2.9	3.0	3.8

1. Data for 1990 are preliminary.
2. Nominal health-care expenditures divided by the GDP deflator.
3. Medical price deflators for personal health care divided by the GDP deflator.
4. Nominal expenditure divided by medical price deflators for personal health care.
Source: OECD.

1980s. Most countries have experienced little relative price growth on average since 1970. Hence, relative price growth of about 2½ per cent per year sets the United States apart from the other six largest OECD countries.[41] However, as noted above, it is very difficult to measure changes in the quality of health care, so that comparisons of the growth of the volume and price of health care across countries may be fraught with considerable statistical inaccuracy.

In 1990, health-care expenditures absorbed about 12.1 per cent of GDP in the United States, compared with about 9.3 per cent in Canada, 8.1 per cent in Germany, and 7½ per cent for the OECD on average. Total nominal per capita health-care expenditures exceeded $2 500 in the United States in 1990, well above Canada, the next biggest spender ($1 770, converted into US dollar at GDP purchasing power parities) and more than twice the average in other OECD

Diagram 20. **OECD HEALTH-CARE EXPENDITURES**
As percentage of GDP[1]

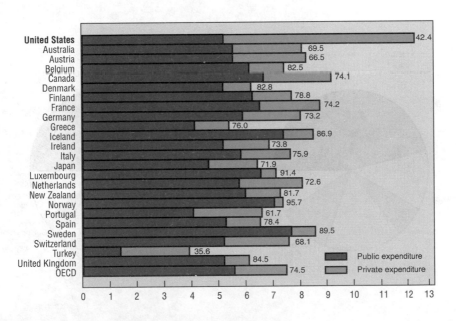

1. Numbers at right are the public sector shares in total health expenditure
Source: OECD, *National Accounts.*

95

Diagram 21. **WHERE THE MONEY GOES**
Selected OECD countries[1]

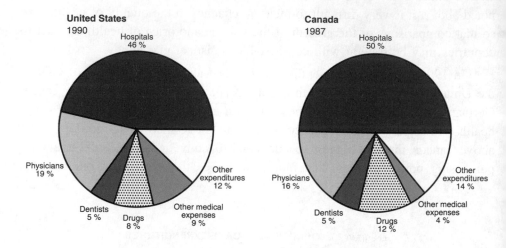

United States
1990

Hospitals
46 %

Physicians
19 %

Dentists
5 %

Drugs
8 %

Other medical
expenses
9 %

Other
expenditures
12 %

Canada
1987

Hospitals
50 %

Physicians
16 %

Dentists
5 %

Drugs
12 %

Other medical
expenses
4 %

Other
expenditures
14 %

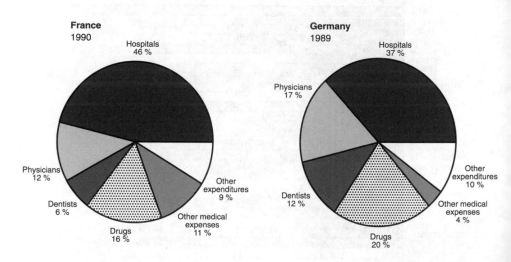

France
1990

Hospitals
46 %

Physicians
12 %

Dentists
6 %

Drugs
16 %

Other medical
expenses
11 %

Other
expenditures
9 %

Germany
1989

Hospitals
37 %

Physicians
17 %

Dentists
12 %

Drugs
20 %

Other medical
expenses
4 %

Other
expenditures
10 %

1. Hospitals include nursing home care.
Source: OECD.

countries, of $1 200. It is well-known that per capita health expenditures rise with per capita income and, to this extent, it is not surprising that the United States ranks the highest in health spending, as it also has the highest per capita income. Nevertheless, U.S. health expenditures are more than one-third higher than the $1 790 that would be predicted by a simple linear income-expenditure relationship across other OECD countries.[42]

As is the case with the growth of expenditures over time, the relatively high level of expenditures in the United States does not appear to be concentrated in any single part of the heath-care system. The share of total health-care outlays going to hospitals, physicians and so forth in the United States is not markedly different from that in other OECD countries. However, the U.S. share of physician services is at the high end of the four countries examined in Diagram 21 (the United States, Canada, Germany and France), whereas the share of expenditures

Diagram 22. **PURCHASING POWER PARITY MEDICAL-CARE PRICES: 1990**
OECD excluding United States = 100

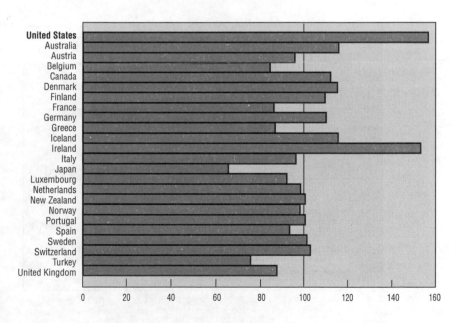

Source: OECD.

97

devoted to pharmaceuticals is substantially smaller in the United States than elsewhere. Since the data are not fully comparable across countries, it is unclear how significant these apparent differences are. But international comparisons suggest that spending appears to be less well controlled across the board (except for pharmaceuticals before the 1980s) in the United States than in other OECD countries.

High U.S. expenditures compared with other countries appear to reflect higher prices to a larger extent than higher volumes, though, as noted above, it is difficult to measure health-care quality. Cross-country comparisons of prices and quantities can be made using purchasing-power-parity (PPP) price indices that are specific to health care, in much the same way as the relative price indices allow one to decompose expenditures over time.[43] By such measures, the U.S. price of health care is the highest in the OECD, 58 per cent above the average in

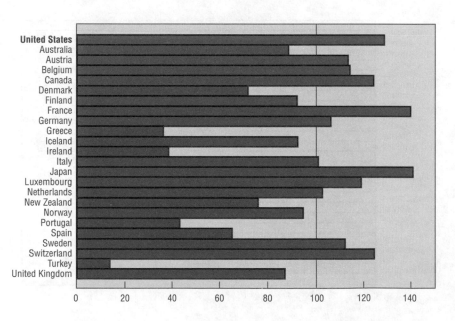

Diagram 23. **VOLUME OF HEALTH-CARE: 1990**
Per capita, OECD excluding United States = 100

Source: OECD.

98

other OECD countries (normalised to 100 in Diagram 9). Dividing expenditures by the PPP prices provides a cross-country measure of the volume of health care. The United States has volumes about 30 per cent greater than the OECD average excluding the United States. This is similar to Switzerland and a bit higher than Canada. By contrast, France and Japan have volumes about 10 per cent higher than the United States.

There is no obvious relationship between number of physicians and health-care costs per capita across OECD countries, and in any case, the number of physicians per capita in the United States is near the OECD average. However, there is a clear cross-country relationship between physician income and per capita health-care expenditures across countries, and compensation per physician is much higher in the United States than in virtually all other OECD countries,

Diagram 24. **HEALTH-CARE EXPENDITURES AND THE NUMBER OF PHYSICIANS PER CAPITA**

1990

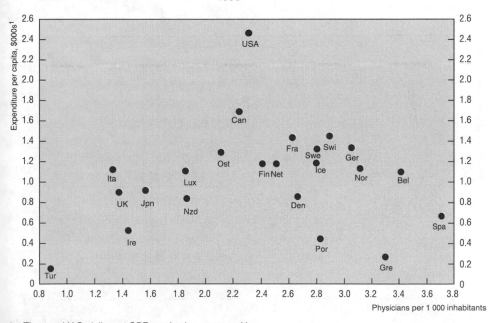

1. Thousand U.S. dollars at GDP purchasing power parities.
Source: OECD.

Diagram 25. **HEALTH-CARE EXPENDITURES AND PHYSICIAN COMPENSATION**
1986/1987

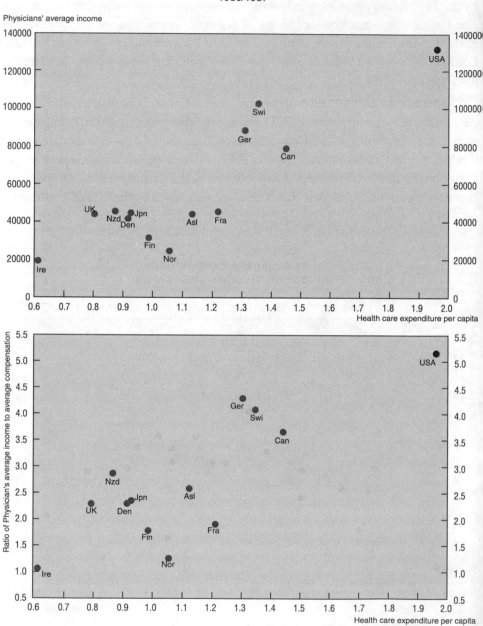

Source: OECD.

whether measured in terms of GDP purchasing power parity, or as a fraction of labour income per worker in the economy as a whole. This suggests that differences in the demand for health services, including the hardness of the overall health-care budget constraint may be as important as factors affecting the supply of physicians – the number of places in medical schools, the cost of receiving training and the stringency of licensing requirements – in accounting for differences in physicians' relative incomes across countries.

Sources of cost pressures

A number of factors have been suggested as contributing to high health-care costs in the United States. This section reviews a number of them, providing a quantitative indication of their importance where feasible.

The pricing of health care

To ensure access, the price consumers pay for medical services is typically far less than the marginal cost in all OECD countries. As a result, demand for services at the margin is generally not limited by the usual market mechanism of requiring purchasers to pay for it. Patients do, of course, bear costs. The average cost, as distinct from the marginal cost, of medical care is covered by taxes and, especially in the United States, by insurance premiums. Patients also pay some of the marginal cost. Services not covered by insurance are paid in full, and many health-care financing systems impose co-payments, deductibles or co-insurance for services that are covered.[44] The U.S. system features high co-payments, relative to those in other OECD countries, which should tend to restrain demand (Manning et al., 1987). However, out-of-pocket expenses have been a rather stable proportion of personal disposable income in the past 20 years, and they have fallen substantially as a proportion of total health-care outlays. Moreover, as discussed below, health-care consumption is highly skewed, and so co-payments, which fall mostly on the first few dollars of expenditure, are an even smaller fraction of the true costs incurred by intensive users of health care. In any case, many people, especially Medicare beneficiaries, purchase extra ''Medigap'' insurance to cover co-payments.[45]

Given the low prices they face, patients have an incentive to overconsume health care. Providers have little incentive to limit supply either, since physicians are morally obliged to provide the best treatment available, they know their insured patients can afford even expensive procedures, and they seek to avoid being sued for malpractice. Thus, the very existence of insurance has led to an increase in the demand for, and the supply of, medical services.[46] Payers, by contrast, do have an incentive to hold costs down, and in the United States private insurers attempt to do so in several ways. They increasingly stipulate "utilisation controls", such as pre-approval, physician review and second opinions, in order

---

Moral hazard and adverse selection

Pure insurance would indemnify people against risks over which they have no control and would be priced to reflect the risk insured against. However, insurance can change the behaviour of the insured so as to increase the risks. This is known as moral hazard. There are also asymmetries of information between the sellers and buyers of insurance that may result in the pool of insured having too high a risk for the price charged for a policy. This is known as adverse selection. Moral hazard and adverse selection undermine pure insurance and, in some circumstances, can even render a competitive insurance market unviable.

Moral hazard occurs if those insured change their behaviour – for example, by consuming more health-care services than they genuinely need, or by devoting less effort to preventive practices – and thereby increase the risk to the insurer. The presence of moral hazard implies that insurance distorts incentives and leads to overly risky behaviour. If insurers could easily distinguish "warranted" from "unwarranted" claims – that is, those events that would have occurred even if insurance had not existed – a policy could be written to cover only the former, and there would be no moral hazard. Some commentators in the health-care field have extended this narrow concept of moral hazard to embrace the idea that the near-zero price for medical care at the margin under a typical insurance policy expands the demand for services.

Adverse selection may arise if individual policy-holders differ in their riskiness (even if there is no moral hazard) and if the insurer cannot fully distinguish differences in their riskiness and hence price policies accordingly. An insurer suffers from adverse selection if the policies it offers attract a disproportionate number of bad risks. Since this would reduce profits, insurers in a competitive market have a strong incentive to avoid adverse selection. Put differently, insurers have an incentive to "cream skim", that is, to attract only relatively low-risk customers if they are not allowed to base their pricing on risk. If, on the other hand, insurers charge premiums based on their assessment of individual risk, then problems of adverse selection can be alleviated. But in the context of health care, this would imply charging the highest premiums to those who need the most care, conflicting with the social goal of equal access.

In contrast to moral hazard, adverse selection does not raise the aggregate risk in a given population (say, everyone in the United States) but simply redistributes the risk across insurers.

to reduce care deemed unnecessary. Since many procedures are elective, patients have the possibility of insuring themselves (or of purchasing more comprehensive and generous policies) only when they know they will have high expenses, an example of adverse selection (see the accompanying box). To reduce these adverse selection problems, insurers often require waiting periods before insurance takes effect and sometimes disallow coverage for pre-existing conditions. However, these practices have reduced access and may also be an impediment to labour mobility. They are therefore likely to be increasingly restricted by law.

It is undoubtedly true that the low marginal cost to patients of services means that substantially more is spent on health care than would otherwise be the case. It is difficult, however, to gauge to what extent such expenditure is excessive. After all, health insurance exists partly to enable people to receive services that they would not otherwise be able to afford – that is, to widen access. At the same time, utilisation reviews and other measures are used by both government and private insurers to counter the incentives to over-use services, in order to offset the effects of low prices. Although their effectiveness is hard to measure, there is some evidence that utilisation management has reduced cost increases while maintaining health-care quality.

Technology

The last few decades have seen revolutionary changes in medicine, which have led to substantial improvements in health care. In some cases – out-patient corneal replacements, for example – the result has been lower costs. On balance, however, costs have risen as the introduction of new techniques – CAT scanners, renal dialysis, coronary by-pass surgery and a host of others – have opened new, often expensive, avenues of diagnosis and treatment. Anecdotal evidence suggests that the trend towards ever-more costly medical technology is continuing and even accelerating. Moreover, it is clear that the diffusion of new medical technology (as measured, for example, by the number of CAT scanners per capita) is much greater in the United States than elsewhere, which is consistent with the much higher level of medical expenditures in this country. These innovations have undoubtedly improved health outcomes, although surprisingly little is known about this, either in the United States or in other OECD countries. In any case nobody would now be satisfied with the medical technology that existed, say, three decades ago.

But medicine is not unique, or even unusual, in having undergone rapid technological change: in consumer durables, aircraft, communications, agriculture, publishing and many other sectors, both the production processes and the products themselves have evolved significantly as a result of the introduction of new technologies. In these sectors, however, technological change has more often been associated with lower, rather than higher, costs. While this divergence between medicine and other industries may reflect differences in technical possibilities – that is, for some reason, improvements in medical techniques tend naturally to be cost increasing – it seems likely that the funding of health-care is a factor.[47] Market forces tend to promote cost-reducing innovation because consumers will buy the least expensive product, all else equal. This is far less true in health care, because practically any non-experimental procedure is covered under almost all insurance plans, and therefore, once an innovation is shown to be even marginally effective, its market is assured almost regardless of cost.

Physicians

There has been considerable scrutiny of the role of physicians in increasing health care costs. In the United States, both health-care expenditures and the number of physicians have risen in tandem, and state health-care expenditures are related to the number of physicians in the state (General Accounting Office, 1992). Moreover, doctors' incomes relative to average incomes are much higher than in other major OECD countries. These observations have led to the hypothesis that physicians are the driving factor behind rising health-care expenses. On the other hand, as noted above, there is little visible relationship across countries between the number of physicians and health-care expenditures. In the United States, expenditures on physician care do not appear to have been particularly responsible for the increase in costs, as they have been fairly stable as a share of total health expenditures. Physician incomes are high, but until recently have been fairly stable as a fraction of average labour income.

Fee-for-service payment, which is widespread in the United States as well as some other OECD countries, provides an incentive to physicians to expand supply. They are able to do so easily because neither patients nor third-party payers are in a position to evaluate their medical decisions. The evidence, though somewhat mixed, suggests that fee-for-service does raise expenditures. Medical-care expenditures tend to be higher in those countries with extensive fee-for-service payment of physicians (the United States, Canada and France, for example). Although Japan has both fee-for-service payment and low expenditures, and thus would appear to be a counter-example, the low expenditures seem to be due to tight price controls and volumes to be rather high (Ikegami, 1991). In the United States, health maintenance organisations (HMOs) that pay doctors on salary have significantly lower costs than fee-for-service insurers. This does not appear to have led to less patient satisfaction with HMOs; it has been traced to less hospitalisation, which is partly attributable to healthier patients, rather than to lower levels of physician services (Manning *et al.*, 1987).

Physicians may also have a substantial indirect influence on health-care expenditures through their role as users and promoters of technology. They have legal and moral obligations to adopt techniques that may improve their patients' health, even if they are very costly and the expected benefit is small. The tort system reinforces these incentives. They also have a financial incentive, since with fee-for-service payment, doctors' incomes rise with the number and sophistication of procedures undertaken.[48] Moreover, physicians often own advanced equipment. Those who own CAT scanners, for example, tend to prescribe more scans, either because they are specialised in patients needing scans or because they wish to increase their incomes. For all these reasons, physicians will choose to work with the best technology, a preference which leads to pressure on hospitals to invest in the latest equipment, and on insurers to cover the best techniques and drugs. This "competition" for physicians, while leading to widespread availability of technology, may also be an important channel for pressure on health-care costs.

Malpractice law

Malpractice suits have drawn criticism as a factor raising health-care costs, and the February 1992 Administration reform proposal suggested changes to limit awards. However, malpractice payouts and premiums, which have tended to decline in recent years, are less than one per cent of health expenditures, although they are more significant for some specialties, such as obstetrics. Thus, malpractice costs cannot directly account for more than a tiny amount of the huge increase in health-care expenditures, even if they rose from nothing only 20 years ago. They probably have had an indirect effect, however, by encouraging "defensive medicine" – excessive diagnostic testing, for example. Estimates of the costs of defensive medicine are naturally very difficult to make, but an upper bound appears to be about 10 to 20 per cent of physician costs, or the equivalent of 2 to 4 per cent of total health-care expenditures. Based on these estimates, malpractice reform is likely to have a non-negligible effect on the level of overall health-care expenditures. Moreover, malpractice reform would improve access to care for certain groups and for certain services physicians are not providing in the current environment.

Waste and unnecessary medical care

There are large variations in medical practice that cannot be explained by variations in incidence of disease, and do not appear to be related to variations in outcomes (see, for example, McPherson, 1990 and Chassin *et al.*, 1987). Practice variation is extremely high in the United States, although there is some evidence that it is also substantial in other OECD countries. In response, a large programme of health-outcome studies has recently been launched in an effort to identify the best practices, and insurance companies have increasingly turned to utilisation controls to monitor care. Practice variation is often seen as evidence for excessive provision of health-care services by physicians and thus as a cause of high expenditures. However, too little is known about diagnosis and treatment to determine the extent to which departures from best practice are responsible for the higher health-care outlays in the United States than elsewhere.

Studies to determine the relationship between alternative treatments and health outcomes are underway. One hope is that eventually clinical guidelines (recommended courses of diagnosis and treatment of specific conditions) can be developed, against which payers can judge the actions of physicians. But these studies are time consuming, expensive and often inconclusive. Moreover, given rapid advances in medical techniques, they are often rendered obsolete by new methods of diagnosis and treatment. These considerations suggest that significant cost savings from regulating care at the micro level are not likely to be realised in the near future. To the extent they were realised, any savings would have to be offset against the costs of the ongoing research and the administrative costs of the utilisation controls themselves.

Administrative and overhead costs

Overhead costs are far higher in the United States than in other OECD countries, owing to high administrative costs associated with the U.S. private-sector insurance industry. (The administrative costs of Medicare and Medicaid are similar to those of public programmes in other OECD countries.) These costs stem from marketing insurance policies, determining eligibility for insurance, and verifying and processing claims. That is, they are the normal costs of providing insurance in a competitive market.

Quantitative estimates of insurance overhead vary widely. Woolhander and Himmelstein (1991) estimate that they ranged from 10 to 13 per cent of personal health-care expenditures in 1987, which, by extrapolation, would be $59 to $76 billion in 1990. The estimate by the General Accounting Office (1991b) was 5.3 per cent in 1990, or $31 billion. Both estimates compare current costs in the United States with what they might be under a Canadian-style public single-payer system. They underestimate the full overhead costs, however, by ignoring the expenses of providers, who must deal with paper work, "utilisation controls" and so forth, and of firms who must shop for insurance policies for their employees. In Canada and in many other OECD countries, overhead is low because: competition among insurers is essentially non-existent, eliminating marketing and shopping costs; payers have no leeway in deciding who and what to cover, eliminating costs of determining eligibility; and payment is according to standardised rate schedules, reducing the claim-processing costs of both providers and payers.

On the other hand, many of the administrative costs that are assumed not to be present in a single-payer system are associated with cost and expenditure controls, including patient payments through deductables and utilisation review programmes. The estimates cited above do not account for the increased utilisation that would occur if these controles were discontinued. For example, a recent study by Shiels et al.(1992) suggests that the higher administrative expenses in the United States relative to Canada may have been associated with at least as important a reduction in utilisation and medical expenditures.

Population ageing

A final factor which has generated increased cost pressures in the health-care system is the steady rise in the share of the elderly in the population. Those

65 and over represented 12 per cent of the total in 1990, compared to only 8 per cent in 1960. Since the elderly require about four times as much health care as the rest of the population, such demographic factors may have been responsible for an increase in health spending of almost ¾ percentage point per year since 1967 (Warshawsky, 1991*b*).

Access to health care

The issue of access can be thought of in two ways. The first is the availability of physical access to the physicians, nursing staff, hospitals, equipment, drugs and so forth needed to deliver care. This is not generally a concern in OECD countries, although in some there have been queues for certain procedures and resources can be scarce in rural areas. The second, more pertinent, dimension of access is the affordability of health care. Health care can be expensive, and those who need it often need a great deal of it. In the United States, half the population consumed 96 per cent of health-care services in 1980, and 5 per cent consumed about half the services (Aaron, 1991). This distribution reflects the skewed pattern of illness in the population. For example, expenditures for the disabled are 5 times more than those on the non-disabled, the old use far more medical services than the young, and medical costs rise very sharply shortly before death (Lubitz and Prihoda, 1984; Congressional Research Service, 1990*c*). It does not appear that this skewed distribution of expenditures is a product of the U.S. health-insurance system, as it was virtually the same in 1929 and is similar in other OECD countries.

In response to the high cost of health care and the disproportionate burden borne by a relatively small fraction of the population, governments of all OECD countries have established programmes to subsidise health care extensively, often to the point where it is free to the individual. In most countries, virtually everyone is covered, typically through mandatory or universal programmes run by public or quasi-public agencies and financed through taxes (although these are often described as ''contributions''). While no such programme covers all conceivable medical procedures, all cover what most people would accept as normal and necessary health care. As noted earlier, individuals in some OECD countries purchase complementary insurance to fill in the gaps in their coverage and to make co-payments. Programmes vary widely in terms of the co-payments required of the patient: the United Kingdom and Canada are at the low end, with virtually no deductibles and co-payments for services covered by their public programmes, and France is at the high end, with co-payments sometimes exceeding 20 per cent (U.S. co-payments are also very high, about 23 per cent of all health-care expenditures).

By contrast, the U.S. health-care financing system is a mixture of private insurance, which covers the bulk of those under 65 years of age, and public programmes having strict eligibility requirements, such as age (in the case of Medicare) or income and family status (in the case of Medicaid). Private insurance is typically purchased by employers on behalf of their employees from private firms which charge premiums largely based on actuarial risk, or provided by employers who self-insure (often using the services of private insurance companies to handle administration). The practice of employer-provided insurance is encouraged by the tax deduction received by employers for the full amount of health-insurance costs (which would not be received by employees if they paid their own premiums). Insurance is also sold to individuals, but the cost is generally much higher than group plans, and individual insurance applicants are carefully screened by insurers to control adverse selection. At any given time, about 15 per cent of those under 65 years of age, or about 13½ per cent of the entire population (some 35 million people), have no insurance coverage at all, either because they are not eligible for public programmes, are not covered by employer group plans, or cannot afford, or choose not to purchase, individual insurance (Congressional Budget Office, 1991*b*).[49]

The principal factor underlying the lack of complete insurance coverage in the United States is the voluntary nature of the health insurance system for those under 65, and its close link to employment. Private insurers have a powerful incentive either to charge bad risks their (high) actuarial cost, or to refuse coverage. In the case of health insurance, the bad risks are those most likely to become ill and incur large medical costs. From the insurers' point of view, proper risk assessment and pricing raises profits and helps control adverse selection problems. From the perspective of the social policy of promoting access to health care, however, the same behaviour is condemned as "cream skimming" and results in gaps in insurance coverage. Those Americans over 65 are covered by Medicare, and virtually everyone in other OECD countries is covered by insurance programmes run by government or quasi-government agencies. Enrolment in all these cases is automatic, and the "insurer" – the governmental agencies – cannot refuse coverage. Hence, the problem of "cream skimming" does not exist.

To some extent, employer-provided group insurance has been successful in dealing with this problem. At least for larger employers, the number of enrollees is high enough that individual risks can be pooled, and the decision to take a particular job, and thereby become insured, is probably largely unrelated to current or prospective health status (although in some industries, the average job risks are so high that insurance coverage can be very difficult to obtain (Aaron, 1991)). The same is much less true of small employers, or of individual insurance policies, and insurers tend to charge high premiums to small firms and individuals because there are fewer policy-holders over which to pool risk. In principle, an insurer could form a large pool by lumping together many small firms or individuals and charging the actuarially fair premium for the group. But if their competitors bid away those policy holders having lowest risks (younger ones, or those with no history of disease, for example), the insurer would suffer from adverse selection – the average riskiness of the remaining pool would rise. It could try to compensate by raising premiums, but this would only chase away more of the low-risk policy holders.

In view of the importance of employer-based insurance, it is not surprising that those having only weak connections to the labour market have a high probability of being uninsured. The unemployed are more than twice as likely as the average to be uninsured (that is, in Table 25, 31.9 per cent of the unemployed were uninsured, compared with 13.6 per cent of the population as a whole); part-time workers are also substantially more at risk; and young adults, who are no longer covered by their parents' insurance but have not yet established careers, are almost twice as likely to be uninsured as the average, although health risks in this group are likely to be low. Labour market connection is, in turn, statistically related to other characteristics: those with family incomes below twice the poverty level are more likely to be uninsured, as are members of minority groups.

Although the percentage of the employed who are uninsured is about the same as that for the general population, four-fifths of all uninsured are in families where the head of the household or the spouse is employed and in nearly 60 per cent of these households, at least one person is employed full time (more than 34 hours per week). The employed are usually uninsured because their employer

Table 25. **Characteristics of the uninsured, 1990**

	Number (Millions)	As a percentage of category	As a percentage of all uninsured
Total uninsured	33.4	13.6	100.0
Age			
Children	8.5	13.3	25.6
Young adults (18-24)	6.4	25.1	19.0
Elderly (over 64)	0.3	1.0	0.9
Family income			
Below poverty line	9.6	30.2	28.8
1-2 times poverty line	10.6	23.3	31.8
2-3 times poverty line	5.9	13.3	17.7
Over 3 times poverty line	7.2	5.9	21.7
Family work status [1]			
Employed	28.6	13.9	80.2
Unemployed	2.0	31.9	6.1
Out of labour force	4.6	9.8	13.7
Hours worked in family [2]			
None	8.8	14.4	26.3
1-24	2.0	26.3	6.1
25-34	2.7	25.8	8.1
Over 34	19.9	11.9	59.5
Race			
White	25.9	12.5	77.5
Black	5.8	19.2	17.5
Other	1.7	19.1	5.0

1. A family is "employed" if either the head of household or the spouse is employed; it is "unemployed" if neither is employed and one is unemployed; it is "out of the labour force" if neither is in the labour force.
2. Hours worked in survey week by the head of household or spouse, whichever is greater.
Source: Congressional Budget Office (1991*b*).

does not offer health insurance and they cannot afford, or will not pay for, an individual insurance policy. In some cases, households are not eligible for coverage under an employer plan because of provisions that, for example, exclude coverage for pre-existing conditions. A few households choose not to enrol in employer plans for individual reasons.

Whether an employer provides insurance or not is related to the firm's size and its industry. Small firms are much less likely to provide insurance than large ones, and there appears to be a trend for businesses to eliminate this benefit in order to avoid the burden of rising health-care premiums.[50] Workers in manufacturing are the best covered, while those in some, but not all, service industries or in other industries with small firms are relatively poorly covered. Cost is a significant factor behind this pattern of coverage. Since small firms and those in service industries tend to pay lower than average wages, insurance premiums, which are a lump sum rather than proportional to wages, raise their labour costs disproportionately.[51] Administrative costs are much higher for small-firm policies – for firms with fewer than 10 employees, administrative costs are up to 40 per cent of benefits paid, compared with only 5 per cent for very large firms. Lastly, as described above, risk pooling is more difficult for small firms, and therefore premiums can be much higher if the insurer expects future claims to be high because, for instance, one employee has a bad medical history.

The proportion of the under-65 population that is uninsured rose by some $2\frac{1}{2}$ percentage points during the 1980s (Congressional Budget Office, 1991b). The reasons for this trend have been difficult to pin down. The unemployment rate rose in the early 1980s, but the proportion of uninsured did not fall with subsequent decline in the unemployment rate. Service-sector jobs increased as a fraction of total employment, but the size of increase and sectoral difference in coverage rates is not sufficient to explain much of the rise in the proportion of uninsured (Congressional Budget Office, 1991b). The share of part-time employees, often not beneficiaries of such fringe benefits, has tended to decline during the 1980s. Analysis by the Congressional Research Service (1988a) points to demographic changes that increased the proportion of young adults, who tend to have weak labour-market ties and better health and are thus poorly covered. If so, coverage should begin to rise again as the "baby-boom" generation ages. On the other hand, the rising costs of insurance will continue to make it less affordable particularly for small employers and individuals.

Those without insurance do not necessarily go without medical care. Some pay for it out of pocket. Those who cannot afford to do so can receive "uncompensated care" from hospitals and have access to public hospitals, usually through the emergency department.[52] However, emergency-department care is an expensive way to deliver health care, and its quality is widely thought to be below the standard received by the insured. It is expensive because emergency rooms are costly, specialised facilities that are not well designed to provide primary care. It also appears that the uninsured tend to go to hospitals rather late in the course of an illness, and therefore require expensive treatment that could have been avoided with earlier medical intervention. Several studies suggest that while the uninsured receive care, it is inferior to that received by the insured.[53] The situation of the uninsured is precarious and could deteriorate if budget restrictions reduce the number of public hospitals, which would in turn reduce access and health status for some people (Bindman *et al.*, 1991), or if for-profit hospitals, which provide less uncompensated care than do non-profit hospitals (Lewin *et al.*, 1988), expand at the expense of non-profit hospitals.[54]

Being without health-care insurance imposes substantial potential and actual costs, both financially and in terms of the quality and quantity of care received. For those not eligible for government programmes, a change in employer, a loss of employment or even a change in the health status of a family member could result in a sharp reduction in coverage, a complete loss of coverage, or much higher insurance premiums. As a result, even the large majority who are covered is bound to factor health insurance into a broad range of economic and social choices – changing employment or family status, for example. Although quantitative estimates of the economic cost of, for example, "job lock" are unavailable, there are certainly deadweight costs stemming from the potential and actual gaps in coverage and the associated risk of losing coverage. As cost pressures and awareness of the problem mount, these deadweight costs could rise.

Health-policy reform

There is now an almost unanimous sentiment that the U.S. health-care financing system is unsatisfactory, and there are disturbing signals that it may be unsustainable.[55] Costs are high and rising, apparently with no limit in sight. There are fears that employers, insurers and governments will respond to the escalation of costs by paring back coverage, thereby eroding access. A significant number of people who already have no health insurance receive relatively poor health care, and some are exposed to potentially crippling financial costs should they fall ill. The diffuse nature of the cost increases and the complex nature of health care and health-care markets have obscured the fundamental sources of the problem. This, together with the diverging interests of the current stakeholders – providers, insurers, employers and various groups of consumers – has resulted in considerable disagreement on how best to reform the system.

The Administration's "Comprehensive Health Reform Plan"

In February 1992, the Administration published its proposal to build on the current health-financing system by retaining, and enlarging, the role of private-sector insurance. Access would be expanded by offering tax credits and deductions, and by reforming the private-sector insurance market. The Plan would leave the current health-care financing system intact: those not covered by Medicare or Medicaid would still be covered by private insurers, mostly through employer group plans.

Tax credits and deductions

All eligible individuals or families – those not already eligible for existing government health-care programmes, such as Medicare and Medicaid – with incomes below the poverty line would receive the maximum tax credit ($1 250 for individuals, $2 500 for a married couple and $3 750 for a family) with which to purchase health insurance. As income rose, the tax credit would fall to a minimum of 10 per cent of the maximum credit at $1\frac{1}{2}$ times the poverty line. Instead of the credit, those eligible could claim a tax deduction if they wished. This would reduce their taxable income by the same amounts as the tax credits and would be phased out at higher income levels (between $40 000 and $50 000 for individuals, $55 000 and $65 000 for couples and $70 000 and $80 000 for families).

The amounts of the credits and deductions correspond to the Administration's estimate of the cost of a "basic" health-insurance policy, although it would be left to state governments to define such a policy and to ensure that private-sector insurers offer it. States would also have the option to fold Medicaid into the tax-credit programme and, in effect, offer tax credits to all the poor. According to Administration estimates, the credits and deductions would extend health-insurance coverage to about 24 million people, or 70 per cent of the currently uninsured.

Insurance reform

All insurers selling group health insurance in a state would be required to sell a policy to any employer group that applies and would have to cover every employee in an insured group. Insurers choosing to cover recipients of tax credits would be prohibited from denying coverage on the basis of health. Insurers would be required to renew policies, unless premiums are not paid or there is fraud. They would be prohibited from limiting coverage on the basis of pre-existing conditions, a measure designed to increase the portability of insurance from job to job. Employers would not be required to provide group insurance or, if they provided it, to contribute to its cost. There would be no government controls on the premiums insurers could charge, except during a 5-year transition period in the case of policies sold to small firms.

Each state would define one or more "basic benefit packages" to be offered by private insurers. If fewer than two insurers in any state offered the basic packages, the

(continued on next page)

(continued)

state insurance commissioner would be able to force two or more of them to do so. Although insurers would be able to charge the market price for the basic-plan premium, the intention is that the plan be designed so its cost equals the maximum tax credit amount. States would not be allowed to mandate benefits (apart from the basic benefit package), nor to restrict the development of co-ordinated care organisations, such as HMOs.

States would implement "health risk pools". Insurance companies and plans covering a group with more unhealthy individuals than average would receive money from the pools, while those covering a healthier than average group would be required to pay into the pools. The intention is to offset the incentive for "cream skimming" by subsidising and taxing insurers according to the health characteristics of those they cover.

Small employers would be encouraged to pool their purchasing power via "health insurance networks", which would operate as non-profit intermediaries. The main encouragement would be that the networks would be exempted from state-mandated benefits and premium taxes. Pooling would reduce the high administrative costs now associated with small-firm insurance.

Cost control

The proposal aims at controlling costs through greater use of co-ordinated care, malpractice reform, and administrative savings through the use of electronic billing and standardised formats. The Plan does not require insurers to harmonise coverage and rate schedules (i.e. does not require a so-called all-payer billing system). The Administration notes that much illness could be reduced through the adoption of healthier life-styles, and that the FY 1993 budget has increased funding for programmes aimed at disease prevention and at care for women and children (nutritional assistance, the head start educational programme and access to primary health care centres). According to the Administration, the measures in the Plan would reduce health-care costs by 6 to 14 per cent in 1997. Using the Sonnefeld *et al.* (1991) projections of health-care costs, this would be $76 to $177 billion.

There is, however, no shortage of suggestions. Several academics have put forward proposals, of which Enthoven's (1980 and 1988, for example) "managed competition" has been particularly influential: recent health-care reforms in the Netherlands and the United Kingdom incorporated some of his ideas. At the federal level, the Administration published a proposal in February 1992, which is described in the accompanying box, and 40 comprehensive health-care reform bills (as distinct from bills targeted to specific populations) were put forward in the 102nd Congress (Congressional Research Service, 1992*b*). There have also been initiatives at the state level, including the Garamendi proposal for California, described in another accompanying box, and the more limited, but highly controversial, Oregon proposal to extend Medicaid coverage to more of the poor while eliminating reimbursement altogether for some procedures.[56]

Containing costs

Any reform that seeks to correct the most glaring problem of the current U.S. system – high and rising expenditures – must effectively restrain demand for services. Care that is almost free, from the point of view of the patient, has set up a dynamic of increased demand, increased supply, and the invention of ever-more sophisticated and costly diagnostic and treatment options. Directly charging consumers (out-of-pocket) the full marginal cost of medical services, the obvious market solution, might provide an effective brake on costs, but is not a serious policy option because it would place health care beyond the financial reach of many people. Thus, mechanisms other than high prices at the point of delivery must be used to balance demand with available resources.

One avenue of reform would be to institute price schedules, quantity constraints and global budgets on all health-care providers. Enforcement of such constraints would be facilitated by a centralisation of health-care finances, as envisaged by proposals for a comprehensive public-sector health-care system put forward by, for example, Congressman Russo and, at the state level, by Mr. Garamendi (see the accompanying box).[57] Reforms such as these would significantly reshape health-care financing in the United States. The role of private insurers would be sharply reduced, and, depending upon the nature of the reform, much of the cost of health-care expenditures might be transferred from the books of the private sector onto government budgets. Private insurers paid over $215 billion for health care in 1990, which would have to be paid by governments and raised through taxes. This would not be a new burden overall, since the taxes would replace insurance premiums. In fact, to the extent that centralised expenditure control permitted reductions in outlays, the burden would fall – one source of saving might be reduced administrative and overhead costs.

Health-care Reform: The Garamendi Proposal

In February 1992, the State Insurance Commissioner of California, John Garamendi, published a proposal to replace the private and public-sector insurance system currently in place in California with universal health-care coverage financed by payroll taxes and delivered by HMO-like managed-care organisations. This would involve a substantial change from the current system, in that employers would no longer be providing, and insurers would no longer be offering, group health insurance plans of the sort that now cover most people under 65 years of age.

Financing

Insurance premiums would be replaced by a payroll tax (referred to as "premiums" in the proposal) of 7.65 per cent on employers and 1.4 per cent on employees, with the self-employed paying the sum of these. To reduce the burden on small firms and low-income workers, in the calculation of their liabilities under the plan, employers would receive a deduction of $10 000 per person, small business would face a lower payroll tax rate and workers would receive a deduction of $5 000. There would be a ceiling of $150 000 per person for income subject to the payroll tax for both employers and employees. According to the Commissioner, the average tax rates would be 6.75 per cent of payroll for firms and 1 per cent for workers.

Regional, autonomous "health insurance purchasing corporations" (HIPCs) would "sponsor insurance", essentially by using the tax revenues to buy medical coverage for all residents (employed or not) from private-sector providers. The effect would be to eliminate the link between employment and health insurance, in that being insured would not depend on being employed, and employees would not be in danger of losing coverage (or, perhaps, even have to change physicians) when they changed jobs.

Access

Each health-care provider organisation would offer plans certified by the HIPC in its area and would be responsible for the actual delivery of medical services. The Proposal envisages basic plans, similar to those now offered by HMOs in California, that would cover in-patient and primary care, prescription drugs, home health care and so forth. Plans would be prohibited from turning down applicants, regardless of past, actual or prospective health status. The HIPC would pay the provider organisation an amount per enrollee, but with adjustments for risk (for example, plans with a disproportionate number of old enrollees would be paid more per head), in order, it is hoped, to prevent "cream skimming" by providers.

Only modest co-payments, and no deductibles, would be permitted. Plans would be allowed to offer more than the basic package certified by the HIPC and would charge their enrollees for the extra services. However, there would be limits on how much more could be offered, for fear that the basic plan might eventually be perceived as sub-standard.

(continued)

The Proposal envisages folding the medical parts of workers' compensation and automobile insurance into the same system, in order to improve access and eliminate duplication of costs.

Cost containment

The major cost-containment mechanism would be the global health-care budget determined by the revenue from the payroll taxes, which will rise no faster than payrolls (unless the payroll tax rates were increased).

According to the Commissioner, the measures in the proposal will hold health costs down by encouraging managed care and by eliminating much of the administrative overhead now incurred by firms and insurance companies. It is also envisaged that the proposed system will be more effective at eliminating unnecessary medical procedures.

However, different people would pay. Because insurance premiums are roughly the same regardless of income, viewed as a tax they are highly regressive. A payroll tax, which is used in many other OECD countries to finance health care, would be roughly proportional to income. Thus, a shift to a comprehensive public health-care programme financed by a payroll tax would tend to shift the cost burden from the low-paid to the better-paid.

Centralised control of health-care budgets is already common in other OECD countries, where health care is financed directly by governments or by quasi-governmental agencies. Many have nation-wide (or, as in Canada, province-wide) fee schedules, to which physicians must adhere when they bill. This approach appears to have been successful in Japan, but in many countries there has been a tendency for providers to increase effort, or to change the way treatment is described in order to collect a higher fee (a practice referred to as upcoding). Similar tendencies have been observed in U.S. government health programmes, and the Health Care Financing Administration built such a response into its recently introduced Medicare Volume Performance Standards. These developments have led some countries to impose both price and quantity targets, or global budgets. The combination of price and quantity controls appears to be more effective in restraining costs than price controls alone (General Accounting Office, 1991*d*).

While centralised budgetary control has provided a mechanism to restrain costs in many countries, it has not eliminated the underlying pressures on expenditures. Thus, in some countries – France and Canada, for example – the share of health-care outlays in GDP is still rising, although the rate of increase has slowed sharply and is well below that in the United States. Generally, centralised expenditure control has not been accompanied by centralisation of delivery of medical care, which has largely remained in the hands of physicians and hospital administrators. Indeed, medical decisions in most OECD countries are typically made by physicians with less supervision and control than has become common in the United States. Likewise, in these countries there are typically fewer restrictions on choice of physician or hospital than is now the case with HMOs or preferred-provider organisations in the United States. On the other hand, centralised budgeting could also lead to a health-care system that is unresponsive to patients' needs. The system in the United Kingdom has been accused of being overly rigid, and its recent reforms were, in part, an attempt to change this (Day and Klein, 1991). Queues for certain surgical procedures, notably coronary surgery, have developed at times in Canada, as financial constraints resulted in a shortage of cardiac facilities. Subsequently this was to some extent corrected (Naylor, 1991).

Some cost-saving reforms have been introduced into U.S. government health-care financing programmes, such as the prospective payment system for hospital Medicare fees introduced in the 1980s and the transition to "diagnosis-related group" (DRG) payments rather than cost-based reimbursement. In 1992, a programme to limit Medicare physician spending was introduced, including a Relative Resource Value Scale, which sets prices for physician services. In an effort to limit physicians' behavioural responses, "volume performance standards" were also introduced. These reforms have stopped short of imposing global budgets, although in its 1992 Budget the Administration raised the issue of capping the growth of Medicare and Medicaid outlays. The impact of such reforms on overall medical outlays would be blunted, however. Providers could compensate for reductions in income received from Medicaid and Medicare by shifting costs to the private sector, as they have in the past when fees under these programmes were reduced, although the extent of this response is subject to considerable debate. In addition, Medicare and Medicaid must compete with the private sector for physician and hospital resources, which limits the amount of restraint that can be imposed without reducing access.

A possible alternative to global budgeting is stricter control over medical costs at the micro level, and, in the absence of a centralised system for collecting premiums and paying providers, the U.S. health-care financing system has moved in this direction. Insurers are increasingly turning to provider-review mechanisms in an attempt to reduce costs. Moreover, the traditional third-party insurer that pays a physician chosen by the patient has been losing ground to managed-care organisations. The standard HMO, for example, provides comprehensive health-care services, usually including hospitalisation, in return for a premium. It is distinguished from other insurers by the close relationship between the insurer and provider: in an HMO they are both of the same company. This type of HMO has significantly lower costs than fee-for-service providers, although the growth of costs has been the same. Other, much looser forms of managed-care organisations, such as preferred-provider organisations, have expanded rapidly in recent years, but appear, at best, to generate only small savings.

Further reform along these lines, as was proposed by the Administration in February, would have the advantage of requiring only incremental changes to the current health-care financing system. Private insurers could retain an important role, although they might more closely resemble HMOs. The efforts of private-sector insurers and the growth of managed care have not yet slowed health-care expenditures, although these efforts have become prominent only in the last decade. As costs continue to rise, insurers will have strong incentives to develop insurance products and care systems that will minimise cost increases.

Access

Although most Americans are covered either by private insurance or by government programmes, about one person in seven is not insured at all, and many others are worried that their coverage may be reduced or eliminated if they lose or change their jobs. The costs of expanding insurance coverage depend on the degree of extension, the generosity of coverage and the health-care demands of those who are now uncovered. An increase in personal health-care outlays of one-seventh would have added about $84 billion to total outlays in 1990, or 1½ per cent of GDP. This figure is, however, a substantial overestimate of the cost of full coverage in that it assumes that those uncovered now use no medical services and that, if covered, they would use the same services as the average person now covered. The uninsured do currently receive care, often at great expense in emergency departments, and when insured would probably use less care than average, because many are young and relatively healthy.

More refined estimates suggest much lower costs. For example, Shiels *et al.* (1992) estimates the cost of providing health care to the currently uninsured to be a substantially lower $11 billion. An extension of employer-based insurance to all firms with 10 or more employees would cut the number of uninsured in half and might raise health-care costs by about $13 to $28 billion, depending on the coverage offered (Congressional Budget Office, 1991*b*). Extending Medicare to provide universal coverage would raise outlays by as much as $26 billion, not allowing for potential savings in administrative costs (Congressional Budget Office, 1991*c*). Expanding Medicaid to cover all those below the federal poverty level would raise outlays by $6 billion, but would not extend insurance coverage much (Congressional Research Service, 1988*b*). To put these figures into perspective, it should be recalled that estimates of the excess administrative cost of private health insurance and the outlay equivalent of the employer tax deduction for health insurance are each on the order of $40 billion. These estimates of the cost of extending health care coverage may be too low, in that they do not consider the possible dynamic pressures that would result from universal, guaranteed coverage. These are, of course, very difficult to assess, but to the extent they emerge, the need to control costs would become even more pressing.

Since gaps in coverage are largely the result of the operation of a voluntary, competitive insurance market, proposals to increase access have centred on reforming, or even replacing, private insurance. Four generic types of reform are now actively being considered in the United States, although, of course, each has many variations.

Small-group insurance reform

Many of the uninsured are employed in small firms that do not offer group insurance, mainly because high risk and administrative costs have made it too expensive. Insurance could be made more affordable for small business by requiring insurers to offer coverage to all firms and to all employees in a firm that has purchased group insurance, and by limiting premiums in some way to prevent insurers from pricing small employers out of the market. This is a conservative reform, in that it implies only a small change to the existing health-insurance system. On the other hand, since this proposal does not require firms to provide insurance to their employees, it is not clear how effective it will be in extending coverage. Moreover, if insurers are forced to provide small-group insurance at below cost, they may choose to withdraw from the market altogether.

Tax credits (or vouchers)

Health insurance could also be expanded by providing individuals with refundable tax credits or "vouchers", which could be used to purchase private health insurance policies, either through employer group plans or directly from insurance companies. The credits could decline with income in order to direct the subsidy more precisely to the poor, and they could be higher for those with serious chronic illnesses, since they are likely to be charged higher premiums.

Although this reform would also leave the current health-financing system largely intact, the degree to which coverage would be expanded would depend on the size of the tax credit and, since there would be no controls on premiums and on coverage by insurers, how the insurance market reacted. Those who do not have insurance would obviously be tempted to buy coverage. It should not change significantly the coverage for those who are now covered by group insurance if the tax credit were a substitute for the tax deduction by employers. Some firms might decide to drop their group insurance, but those employees losing it would buy their own coverage using the tax credit. However, in the absence of insurance reform, vouchers alone would not guarantee that high-risk individuals and groups would not be denied insurance.

Neither small-business insurance reform nor tax credits would entirely resolve the problem of "cream skimming" – insurers would still have a strong incentive to cover those perceived as low risks. These incentives could be offset if the government transferred money from insurers having a low-risk clientele, to those having a disproportionate number of high-risk cases. The Administration proposal, for example, includes such a mechanism. Such compensation would be feasible though not complete. Observable characteristics, such as age, sex and past health status, appear to explain only a small percentage of the variation in health expenses across individuals, though this is all the information that insurers utilise now in setting risk-based premiums. Nonetheless, it may be expensive for a government to duplicate the rating done by insurance companies. An alternative would be to prohibit differences in premiums based on risk, although such an attempt to frustrate a powerful market incentive may prove difficult to enforce. More importantly, it would magnify the incentive for insurers to avoid bad risks by refusing coverage altogether, or by attempting to tailor policies to discourage those who might generate large claims. These practices, too, could be forbidden. But if they could no longer choose whom to insure, the terms of insurance, or what price to charge, the role of insurers would be narrowed to administrative and cost-control functions. The issue then would be focused upon their efficiency in this role: comparisons with public programmes in the United States and elsewhere suggest that private-sector overhead costs are relatively high, while there is little evidence concerning the relative efficacy of the two sectors in controlling health-care costs.

"Play or pay"

Under this option, proposed by some members of Congress, employers could choose to offer a group plan, or to pay a payroll tax to finance a public plan that would cover its employees, perhaps an extension of Medicare or Medicaid. This would extend coverage to the entire employed population. Under some variants, anybody not covered by private insurance would be automatically eligible for the public plan. In this case, access would be universal although some prices might be attached. It is likely that low-wage firms (which would pay little payroll tax) and high-risk people (who would be charged large premiums in the private market) would be most attracted to the public plan.

Initially, it might be expected that private insurers and employers would retain their dominant role as payers. However, health-care costs are rising much faster than payrolls, and if the contribution rate were fixed, more firms would choose to join the public plan over time. This would entail rising transfers from general revenues. Even if contributions were raised in line with costs, a public programme would take an increasing share of the market if it were able to deliver greater consumer satisfaction for less. In either of these cases, "play or pay" could prove to be a transition to a health-care financing system dominated by public-sector payers.

Comprehensive public health insurance

Universal coverage could also be achieved directly by replacing the current mixed public-private insurance system with an entirely public one, which would cover everyone automatically and probably reduce administrative costs. Cost-increasing technological innovation could also slow as well. Of the options discussed, this one would require the greatest changes to the current system, and would also move the U.S. health-care financing system furthest toward those in place in other OECD countries. It would represent a departure from U.S. approaches to such issues in two respects – first in embracing a radical rather than evolutionary approach, and second in forcing the private sector out of an activity where it is established. The experience of other countries suggests that there are many ways to design a comprehensive public system, and the institutions actually in place in those countries have grown up in response to complex cultural, political, economic and social pressures. U.S. solutions will likewise undoubtedly evolve in response to similar pressures.

Concluding remarks

While numerous proposals have been put forward for health-care reform, real options are fewer than they may seem. Gaps in coverage are largely the result of voluntary, competitive insurance markets. And with unusually rapid cost growth, insurance premiums have increased so much that small firms and certain groups of individuals can no longer afford to buy coverage. Improving access to health care while maintaining the current system requires further government involvement in terms of insurance regulation and offsetting income transfers. This tendency towards greater government intervention is likely to intensify if present cost trends continue. On the other hand, experience in other OECD countries as well as in the United States suggests that efforts to contain outlay growth – which will be necessary in any event – inevitably entail greater price and volume controls in health-care delivery, whether through managed care, as is increasingly the case in the United States, or through a centralised government programme, as is the case in most other OECD countries. The real choice is on the financing side: between a regulated private insurance system or a centralised financing system.

VI. Conclusions

The period of slow growth in the U.S. economy which began in 1989 continued through mid-1992. Even though the recession following Iraq's invasion of Kuwait was short-lived, output has increased at a rate of only about 1½ per cent per year over the past three and a half years, clearly less than the economy's supply potential. As a result, the unemployment rate has moved up fairly sharply, recently reaching 7¾ per cent, as job creation has continued to be meagre over the past year of recovery. Employers have thus far remained hesitant to hire, preferring to meet increases in demand by running down inventories and increasing employee overtime and productivity.

There are several reasons for the sluggishness of the recovery thus far, especially when seen in relation to previous historical episodes. First, structural imbalances, although reduced, have probably not been entirely resolved. For businesses, the excesses of 1980s in commercial construction will remain a millstone for the economy for some years to come. On the other hand, corporate balance-sheet restructuring has made substantial progress, and firms should be ready to face the financial implications of their potential investment in plant and equipment. While credit-card debt has fallen sharply, overall household indebtedness has continued to rise, albeit at a much reduced rate. Second, the macroeconomic policy stance has been much less expansionary than is typical in the early stages of a recovery. Fiscal policy, hamstrung by the huge structural deficit, as well as the overhang from the savings and loan bailout, has not provided much support to aggregate demand; indeed, actual and expected defence cut-backs have had a dampening effect on activity in some regions. Short-term interest rates have been cut aggressively to near zero in real terms, but M2 has not responded and in fact declined in absolute terms during the second quarter. Long-term interest rates have fallen only slowly, reflecting, in part, some scepticism on disinflation prospects. Third, unemployment has risen only about half as much as it did in the recessions of 1974-75 and 1980-82; as a result, pent-up demands may be more limited.

The Secretariat projections are that the thus-far sluggish recovery will pick up speed, with output growth attaining 1³/₄ per cent this year and 2 to 2¹/₂ per cent in 1993. Inventories are lean; firms intend to invest heavily in new plant and equipment, and should start hiring again; and exports should continue to benefit from strong competitiveness as well as brisker growth in world trade. Unemployment is projected to have peaked but to remain near 7¹/₂ per cent until end-1993. In the very near term, however, the risks are primarily on the downside: structural-imbalance problems could prove more tenacious, confidence appears shaky and foreign markets may not prove as buoyant as projected. Nevertheless, once the recovery is firmly established, it could be sharper than foreseen, especially given the continuing easing of monetary conditions in response to signs of weak activity.

The obverse side of the hesitant pick-up in activity has been a further slowing in inflation. Twelve-month consumer-price increases have fallen from 5¹/₂ per cent in 1990 to 3 per cent most recently, and while about half of this reduction has been attributable to favourable food and energy price developments, further disinflation is in store over the next year and a half, given the substantial slack in both labour and product markets. The external accounts are also favourable: benefiting from enhanced competitiveness, exports have done relatively well, and the deficit on current account was virtually eliminated in 1991. While the current-account deficit has widened again, due primarily to the cessation of contributions by allies to operation Desert Storm as well as a pick-up in import volumes, it should remain of little immediate concern at around 1 per cent of GDP, far below the 3¹/₂ per cent recorded in 1987.

If real activity picks up as projected, there is no need for macroeconomic policy to give further impetus to the economy. In any case, there is no scope for any fiscal stimulus without compromising all pretence of controlling the Federal budget deficit in the near future. For its part, monetary policy would now appear to have gone about as far as desirable in the direction of easing, given the risk of overstimulation if the impact of interest-rate cuts proves to be only slightly delayed, and a future sharp upward movement in rates is to be avoided. Yet if the recovery were to continue to falter, the monetary authorities would have to respond, all the time keeping in mind the medium-term goal of price stability.

Given the significant reduction in inflation, the opportunity to consolidate this progress should not be missed. Long-term interest rates will come down only to the extent that disinflationary policies are maintained and the permanence of relatively low short-term rates comes to be accepted.

The focus of policy-makers' attention should be clearly on the medium term. It is worrying that real hourly compensation of workers has grown very slowly since 1973 and real hourly wages not at all in the 1980s. Also, net national saving in the second half of the 1980s was only 2½ per cent of GDP, giving reason for concern for future prospects. The most direct contribution government policy can make to ensure future living standards is to address the persistent problem of the Federal budget deficit. The approach the United States has tried in order to tackle the deficit – multi-year plans with little short-term consolidation – has not been sufficient, and further efforts are needed in order to prevent an upward spiral of government indebtedness. Steady downward pressure on expenditure will clearly be necessary; however, it may not be adequate, and in that case tax increases must be considered. It is not difficult to come up with lists of policies that would eliminate the structural deficit. Indeed, adopting policies that are commonplace in other OECD countries could solve the problem by mid-decade. For example, Federal spending on medical care is projected to rise by more than 1 per cent of GDP by 1996, growth which could be reduced by adopting effective cost controls. A modest energy tax of, say, 25 cents per gallon on gasoline could raise substantial revenue, of perhaps $23 billion per year. And a broad-based value-added tax at a 5 per cent rate could reduce the structural deficit by two thirds. Since U.S. taxes are the lowest in the OECD and public health-care expenditures are fairly high, the scope for these solutions is relatively broad. The deficit problem, then, does not stem from lack of obvious solutions. Rather, it is the failure to confront the issue squarely and develop a consensus between the Administration and the Congress on the choices that are available. Until this happens, the United States' prospects for real income growth will be diminished and financing U.S. investment with foreign capital inflows could become increasingly expensive.

Pursuing structural reforms would also enhance the efficiency of the U.S. economy and increase the opportunities for profitable investment. One item on that agenda would be to address weaknesses in education and training in order to confront the demands of the labour market in the 1990s. Two other items

127

– banking reform and trade policy – are discussed at length in this year's *Survey*. In 1991, a limited banking reform law was passed which will help regulators prevent future losses to deposit-insurance funds. But U.S. banking regulation remains among the most restrictive in the OECD in some respects. Reducing restrictions – especially those on interstate branch banking – would strengthen the U.S. financial sector. In addition, trade policy needs to be firmly directed at freer trade. Reliance on existing voluntary export restraints – such as those on automobiles, machine tools and meat – should be eliminated. Attempts to impose unilateral solutions to disputes and to manage trade should be replaced by multilateral approaches to achieving free trade. Further multilateral liberalisation of the world trading system through completion of the current round of GATT talks would support such changes and have important benefits for the United States and the rest of the world. The North American Free Trade Agreement is a welcome development, especially given the complementary relationship with the Uruguay Round negotiations.

In addition, the United States should strive to make its tax system less distorting. While the need to control the budget deficit precludes for now such important reforms as corporate profits tax integration, other measures, such as taxing implicit rents on owner-occupied housing and eliminating the deductibility of benefits such as health insurance (as part of a comprehensive health-care reform – see below), would both raise additional revenues and remove important distortions. Also, raising revenue to reduce the deficit should be done in ways that would help attain other policy goals and encourage savings. Higher gasoline or other energy taxes, for example, would have important environmental benefits, while introducing a national value-added tax would favour saving and investment relative to raising income-tax rates.

But perhaps the most serious structural problem is the health-care system. Health-care expenditures in the United States are far higher than those in other OECD countries and are rising much more rapidly, whether measured in terms of GDP or per capita. While it is difficult to say what levels of spending or growth are optimal, there is a mounting concern about the rising burden of health-care costs. At the same time, one in seven Americans is not covered by health insurance at all, many others are faced with the risk of losing insurance coverage if they become unemployed and yet others hesitate to change jobs for the same reason. This situation, characterised by some as a worsening paradox of excess and deprivation, clearly calls for correction, and there is a broad consensus in the United States that something must be done to improve access and contain excessive spending growth. Views differ widely, however, as to specifically what should be done and how, and numerous reform proposals have been put forward in recent years, including one by the Administration.

It is encouraging that the linkage between health-insurance provision and employment would be weakened under most of the recent reform proposals, even those that would keep the present institutional set-up intact. This linkage is archaic and makes no more sense than linking automobile insurance to people's employment. It restricts the individual's choice of insurance, as employees are effectively obliged to accept any group insurance plan that the employer chooses, thereby limiting the presumed advantage of a decentralised financing system. It also acts as an impediment to labour mobility and is costing the Federal government $40 billion per year in tax subsidies.

The fundamental nature of the problem of health care is common to all countries, and as was pointed out in Chapter V, the real choice facing the United States is rather narrower than it appears. While reforms carried out in several OECD countries have brought about a varying degree of spending restraint, underlying pressures for higher health-care outlays nevertheless remain high everywhere in the OECD area and are likely to grow even stronger in the long term with the ageing of the population. The root cause of such pressures lies in the very nature of the system of health-care provision and financing. Once insured, the incremental cost for a patient of receiving medical treatment is typically very low, whereas physicians have incentives, both moral and financial, to offer as much and as good a treatment as they can. In order to deal with the open-ended nature of health-care outlays, OECD countries have responded by raising the incremental costs borne by the patient as well as by placing some limits on what physicians can charge and deliver. This is also what has been done in U.S. public programmes, and private insurers in the United States have similarly intensified their efforts to keep spending growth under control. There seems to be little choice in reforming the system of health-care delivery but to redirect physicians' incentives towards cost saving by imposing some form of budget constraint under whatever financing system the country may choose to adopt.

A salient feature of the U.S. health-care system is the prevalence of private insurance coverage, even for basic health-care services. Efficient operation of insurance markets inevitably leads to pricing based on risk. But basing insurance premiums on health risk is not compatible with the social goal of providing universal access to comprehensive basic care. Thus, improving access to health care while preserving the existing institutional arrangements will require greater regulation of private insurance, compensation for the difference in risks covered by insurers and, given the very high cost of medical insurance in the United States, income-related subsidies to ease the burden of subscribers. Such a way of extending coverage carries heavy administrative overhead costs. However, it has the advantage that the insurance package can be more easily adapted to individual preferences and needs. The alternative is centralised health-care financing which is found in many OECD countries. This would guarantee universal access, carry lower administrative costs and by its very nature avoid the problem of cream-skimming (a tendency for insurance companies to try to cover only the healthy). Cost control through budgetary constraints could be easier under this system. On the other hand, the individual's choice of basic insurance coverage would be limited, although freedom to choose physicians and hospitals need not be. Centralised financing of basic health-care provision does not preclude supplementary private insurance in order for the individual to extend coverage beyond basic needs. But whatever mix of public and private provision is ultimately chosen, it is doubtful that mere marginal reforms can adequately deal with the problems facing the U.S. health-care system.

To sum up, the conditions are in place for a continuation of the moderate economic recovery underway over the past year. The fragility and uneven pace of the expansion thus far are in large part attributable to private-sector financial imbalances which are in the process of correction. Weak private-sector confidence also appears to have been important. Its restoration will be most readily achieved by steady adherence to the medium-term goal of price stability and by progress in reducing the Federal budget deficit. Combining these with a revival of the reformist spirit in the structural-policy domain provides the surest route to better economic outcomes in the remainder of the 1990s.

Notes

1. One measure of restriction has shown notably less restriction than usual: in some past recessions, commercial paper issuance soared, as firms unable to get loans from banks sought other sources of financing. No such pressure emerged in 1990 and 1991. However, the commercial paper market grew rapidly in the 1980s, and it is possible that a large enough proportion of potential borrowers now rely on the commercial paper market for the bulk of their borrowing that it is no longer useful as an indicator of credit scarcity.

2. Historically, there has been no particular relationship between the saving rate and the business cycle for the United States.

3. Short-term money-market rates were strongly negative in real terms in the 1971, 1976 and 1980 recoveries. Rates were just slightly negative in 1961 and remained positive in real terms in 1983.

4. In related work on the effects of credibility, Englander and Egebo (1992) discuss the consequences of joining the exchange-rate mechanism of the European Monetary System (ERM). They find little evidence that countries joining the ERM have improved their inflation-unemployment trade-off.

5. Comparisons over long periods for this and subsequent analyses are made between the years 1959, 1969, 1979 and 1989. In addition to being spaced at even ten-year intervals, these years all represent similar degrees of resource utilisation, since they are all at or just before cyclical peaks, and so are useful for making comparisons that abstract from the effects of the business cycle.

6. As pointed out by Adams and Chadha (1992), though, this slowing contribution of capital may be an endogenous response to the earlier slowing in multifactor productivity growth.

7. The fixed-price data suffer from substitution bias (Triplett, 1992) which is not present in the nominal share. However, investment goods prices rose more slowly than the GDP deflator during the 1980s, and the nominal share may exaggerate the situation for this reason.

8. Aschauer (1989) has presented econometric results that suggest a much more important role for public-sector investment. However, Ford & Poret (1991) find that this result is not robust over time or across OECD countries.

9. However, other evidence, such as results on standardised tests, suggests that educational achievement of U.S. high-school graduates has been declining steadily for several decades.

10. Adams and Chadha (1992) make a similar argument.

11. See Federal Reserve Board (1992) for a discussion of issues relating to the distribution of wealth.

12. Compositional shifts can be inferred by comparing the employment cost index (ECI) and the other measures because the ECI measures average wages or compensation using fixed occupational and industry employment weights, whereas the other measures simply divide payrolls by the total number of hours worked. The comparison shows that real wages for production workers and total workers as measured by the ECI fell by the same amount over the 1980s, which rules out an explanation that relies heavily on highly paid workers becoming more highly paid, at least within the broad categories being examined here. (This did happen to some extent over the 1980s, but not enough to move up the overall aggregate.) Interestingly, comparing the ECI and non-ECI measures of compensation for all workers, the changing composition does not appear to have made a large difference, since both measures were about flat. However, for production-worker wages, changing composition had an important effect, driving down the average hourly earnings measure relative to the ECI. An explanation that could reconcile these facts is that middle-income jobs were lost over the 1980s, while employment increased in the higher-income non-production-worker group and in the less-well-paying parts of the production-worker category.

13. The asset-based measures look at changes in the stock of assets directly. This approach has the advantage over the income-flows-based approach that it allows changes in the valuation of assets to be captured. This means that depreciation is automatically taken into account. And, if an investment project fails, the asset value falls, but no account is taken in the national accounts. Similarly, if a project is successful and generates large profits, the asset price rises, but national-accounts measures do not capture this effect. Also, adjusting measured saving rates for inflation is particularly easy to do with the asset-based measures.

14. The extent to which the private-sector saving rate moves to offset deficit-reduction measures depends on what action is taken. In a static sense, if deficit reduction comes in the form of spending that has little private-sector substitutability, such as defence, there will be little offset. If, though, the spending cut were to come in the form of lower medical payments to the elderly, then to at least some extent their spending is likely to rise, and the private saving rate will partially offset the government saving increase. Dynamic offsets are also potentially important – saving may rise to offset future tax liabilities, for example – but evidence generally suggests that there would be little private-sector offset (see Nicoletti, 1988).

15. These calculations are based on the central assumptions of a 6 per cent discount rate and productivity growth of ³/₄ per cent per year. The cost to future generations rises with the discount rate and falls with the productivity growth rate. However, it should be kept in mind that generational accounting is experimental and therefore subject to considerable uncertainty.

16. There were two GRH laws, one in effect from December 1985 to September 1987 and requiring budget balance by 1991, the second in effect until November 1990, and promising balance by 1993.

17. Mandatory programmes (also referred to as "entitlement" programmes) are those for which expenditure is not set by legislation but, rather, is determined by eligibility requirements. Most mandatory programmes are transfers. An example is Medicaid, a programme to subsidise health care for the poor – expenditures depend on the number of people who qualify as

"poor" and on their medical claims. Mandatory spending accounts for about half of total federal expenditure.

18. Some Washington wits refer to Social Security as the "third rail" of American politics – touch it and you're dead.

19. Taxing 85 per cent of Social Security benefits would approximate the tax treatment of certain private pensions.

20. Among the administrative complexities would be how a Federal VAT would interact with existing state sales taxes.

21. In 1990, the national accounts estimated imputed rent from owned-occupied housing at $379 billion, or 7 per cent of GDP. From this would likely be deducted $88 billion in estimated housing stock depreciation and $48 billion in other expenses required to produce this rent. Using 20 per cent as a rough estimate of the average marginal tax rate gives potential tax revenue of 0.9 per cent of GDP.

22. In September 1992, the FDIC responded by announcing a plan to increase premiums from 23 cents to an average of 25.4 cents for banks and 25.9 cents for savings and loans per $100 of domestic deposits to take effect in January 1993. The new rates vary from 23 to 31 cents, with 75 per cent of banks and 60 per cent of savings and loans expected to qualify for the lowest rate, thereby avoiding any increase. Thus, in total banks' costs will rise by an estimated $600 million per year, while those of savings and loans will increase by $180 million, hardly enough to repay the Treasury credit line referred to above.

23. In fact, most studies find that economies of scale are exhausted relatively quickly.

24. To the extent that risks to the safety net remain from such linkages, the case is stronger to allow banks to link with other financial firms than with non-financial ones, since the potential efficiency gains from affiliations with financial firms are likely to be stronger than from links with non-financial ones. Such synergies provide a greater offset to the risks created by allowing affiliations.

25. The expiration of VRAs in the steel industry in 1992 will further reduce this share.

26. To avoid the possibility of Congressional amendment an agreement must be concluded by 1 March 1993, so that it may be signed by 1 June, following a 90-day notification period to Congress.

27. The Dunkel text contained a number of highlights pertaining to agriculture: "tarification", that is non-tariff barriers would be converted to tariff equivalents; tariffs would be reduced by an average of 36 per cent from 1986 levels over six years; export subsidies would be cut by 24 per cent from 1986-90 levels over six years; internal support would be lowered by 20 per cent from 1986-88 levels over six years; all countries would guarantee minimum access of foreigners equal to 3 per cent of average consumption in 1986-88.

28. One of the more important is the U.S.-EC meat hormone dispute which has resulted in 100 per cent tariffs on $100 million of U.S. imports from the EC. Another, between the same two entities, is centred on the EC's Utilities Directive.

29. According to the Congressional Budget Office (CBO, 1991d), 69 per cent of U.S. textiles imports and 88 per cent of apparel imports were subjected to quantitative restrictions in 1990.

133

30. This would have the same population and even a slightly larger GDP than the European Economic Area.

31. For a summary of recent research on the effects of the NAFTA on trade, employment and wages in the United States and Mexico, see Hufbauer and Schott (1992, Table 3.4). A recent update of their analysis places net job creation from NAFTA at 175 000. Annex III of the OECD's recent Economic Survey of Mexico contains a detailed examination of the NAFTA from the Mexican perspective.

32. Virtually all Latin American countries have now signed bilateral framework agreements on trade and investment with the United States. Chile would appear to be first in line for a future free trade agreement. This might be detrimental to Canadian interests if such agreements are solely bilateral [the so-called "hub-and-spokes" approach (Wonnacott, 1991)]. However, Canada is likely to benefit from enhanced trade and investment opportunities in Mexico and the rest of Latin America.

33. For example, high infant mortality is closely related to low birthweight, and there are a relatively large number of low-birthweight infants in the United States. This depends more on social factors than on the design of the health-care system.

34. Personal health-care expenditures equal the total less research and development costs, construction, public health expenditures, programme administration and the net cost of private health insurance. The latter spending items amounted to 12 per cent of the total in 1990.

35. There has been continuous invention of new medical techniques and products, as well as improvements in older ones. To the extent that these are not taken into account in the estimates of price, they will show up as lower quantities. For many of the important components of health costs – hospitals and physicians services, for example – this problem is probably no more severe than for other goods and services. On the other hand, it may be important for the application of new technologies. For example, a scanner may provide a better diagnosis than a physical examination or an X-ray, but it also costs more. Trajtenberg (1989) found that computerised axial tomography (CAT) scanners underwent considerable quality improvements shortly after their introduction in the early 1970s.

36. Total, rather than personal, health-care expenditures are used to enable comparisons with other countries in Table 24 below. Data on personal health-care expenditures are not nearly as widely available for other countries. In the case of the United States, using total expenditures instead does not make any material difference.

37. It should be noted, however, that the rate of increase in physician incomes was roughly similar to that of other post-college-educated workers in the late 1980s.

38. Correspondingly, the share of the private sector in the total personal expenditure on health care has declined. This has been entirely due to a fall in the relative importance of out-of-pocket payments: private insurance has covered an increasing part of health-care spending (see Table 23).

39. Rising health-care expenditures have led to a growing wedge between the wage bill and total compensation. Business health-care costs have surged from 3 per cent of total compensation in 1970 to over 7 per cent in 1990. In 1991 these costs amounted to 92 cents per hour worked. Furthermore, this excludes unfunded future liabilities for retiree health-care benefits

which have been estimated to amount to as much as $400 billion in present value terms; beginning in 1993, U.S. accounting rules will force employers to recognise such liabilities.

40. The outlay equivalent is the amount the government would have to transfer to provide the taxpayer with the same after-tax income as is received from the tax concession. It is higher than the revenue lost because the transfer would normally be taxable income, and so some of it would be taxed back.

41. The economics of health-care systems in various OECD countries are discussed in more detail in OECD (1992).

42. Unconstrained demands for health care may be considerably more income-elastic than indicated on Diagram 17. The linear relationship may reflect the role of centralised health-care budgeting in restraining the demand for health care. In the absence of these restraints, the health-expenditure shares of other OECD countries might rise non-linearly, and the U.S. share might not be significantly out of line with that of countries with similar levels of per-capita income.

43. These figures should be used with caution as they are often based on a rather sparse selection of service prices.

44. A *co-payment* is a fixed sum per procedure. A *deductible* is an amount that must be paid (per year, for example) before insurance applies. *Co-insurance* is a percentage of the cost of a service. In what follows, all these will be loosely referred to as co-payments.

45. The purchase of supplemental insurance is not unique to the United States – in France and Canada, 60-70 per cent of the population purchases supplemental insurance.

46. Potentially, insurance may also expand demand by changing behaviour, a problem known as moral hazard (see the accompanying box). An example might be people smoking more, knowing they would be covered by insurance should they become ill. It is not clear that moral hazard, in this sense, is important in the context of health care. Some authors, however, use the term moral hazard in a wider sense to include the increase in demand in response to low prices.

47. Weisbrod (1991) presents an extensive argument along these lines. He provides an interesting comparison between the health-care system and the public education system in the United States. In the former, insurance is open-ended and resource use is determined largely by health-care providers. In the latter, the government provides a fixed amount per student, or families pay the entire cost out of pocket, and resource use is not determined by teachers. This example cuts both ways since most people report satisfaction with their health care, whereas dissatisfaction with the public school system appears to be widespread.

48. Hospital-based physicians in other OECD countries are salaried, unlike in the United States, and may have less financial incentive to require the most recent technology.

49. There are other ways of defining who is uninsured, although the "point-in-time" measure is both meaningful and easily derived from survey data. Two alternative definitions are the percentage of the population having no insurance cover for an extended period of time (say, a year), and the percentage that is uncovered for at least one short spell during an extended period. For example, in the 30-month period from February 1985 to August 1987, 4.3 per cent had no health insurance cover at any time, while 28.1 per cent had at least one one-month spell during which they were uncovered (Aaron, 1991).

50. Between 1979 and 1986 the proportion of those in the labour force who receive health-insurance coverage through their jobs declined by 1.1 percentage points (Congressional Research Service, 1988a).

51. Also, small businesses often face more intense competition and may have smaller profit margins.

52. The result is that hospitals must recover the cost of such uncompensated care through increased charges for other patients – leading to a potential problem of cost shifting – or through state-wide uncompensated care pools.

53. See, for example, Bindman *et al.* (1991), Eisenberg (forthcoming), Lurie *et al.* (1984) and Wenneker *et al.* (1990).

54. This latter possibility may not pose too great a concern. While for-profit hospitals do provide less care to the uninsured, they do so primarily because they are located in areas where there are relatively few uninsured. If this is the case, they are unlikely to expand at the expense of those non-profit hospitals that provide a lot of care to the uninsured.

55. While many Americans feel that big changes are needed in the health-care system (57 per cent), most are at least somewhat satisfied with their own health care (71 per cent) (Harris Poll, June 17, 1992).

56. The Oregon proposal is to reimburse the costs of only the first 587 of 709 different medical treatments, ranked according to medical effectiveness and value to the individual and society. This proposal was denied a Medicare waiver by the Administration in August 1992 on the grounds that it might violate the Americans with Disabilities Act. Other states, such as Florida, Minnesota and Vermont are also in the process of attempting to reform Medicaid with a view to broadening public health insurance.

57. The Garamendi proposal is discussed here for illustrative purposes only.

References

Aaron, H.J. (1991), *Serious and Unstable Condition: Financing America's Health Care,* The Brookings Institution, Washington, D.C.

Adams, C. and B. Chadha (1992), "Growth, Productivity, and the Rate of Return on Capital", IMF Working Paper No. 92-35.

Aschauer, D.A. (1989), "Is Public Expenditure Productive?", *Journal of Monetary Economics,* 23, March, pp. 177-200.

Baily, M.N. and C.L. Schultze (1990), "The Productivity of Capital in a Period of Slower Growth", *Brookings Papers on Economic Activity: Microeconomics,* pp. 369-406.

Bayard, T.O. and K.A. Elliott (1992), "'Agressive Unilateralism' and Section 301: Market Opening or Market Closing?", Xerox, Institute of International Economics, Washington, D.C.

Bindman, A.B., D. Keane and N. Lurie (1990), "A Public Hospital Closes", *Journal of the American Medical Association,* December 12, Vol. 264, No. 22, pp. 2899-2904.

Bindman, A.B., K. Grumbach, D. Keane, L. Rauch and J.M. Luce (1991), "Consequences of Queuing for Care at a Public Hospital Emergency Department", *Journal of the American Medical Association,* August 28, Vol. 266, No. 8, pp. 1091-1096.

Budget of the United States Government, various years.

Chassin, M.R., J. Kossecoff, R.E. Park, C.M. Winslow, K.L. Kahn, N.J. Merrick, J. Keesey, A. Fink, D.H. Solomon and R.H. Brook (1987), "Does Inappropriate Use Explain Geographic Variations in Health Care Services?", *Journal of the American Medical Association,* November 13, Vol. 258, No. 18, pp. 2533-2537.

Congressional Budget Office (1991*a), Rising Health Care Costs.*

Congressional Budget Office (1991*b), Selected Options for Expanding Health Insurance Coverage.*

Congressional Budget Office (1991*c), Universal Health Insurance Using Medicare's Payment Rates.*

Congressional Budget Office (1991*d), Trade Restraints and the Competitive Status of the Textile, Apparel and Nonrubber Footwear Industries.*

Congressional Budget Office (1992*a), The Economic and Budget Outlook: Fiscal Years 1993-1997.*

Congressional Budget Office (1992*b), Reducing the Deficit: Spending and Revenue Options.*

Congressional Budget Office (1992*c), The Economic and Budget Outlook: An Update.*

Congressional Research Service (1988a), *Health Insurance and the Uninsured.*

Congressional Research Service (1988b), *Costs and Effects of Extending Health Insurance Coverage.*

Congressional Research Service (1990a), *Controlling Health Care Costs*, 90-64 EPW.

Congressional Research Service (1990b), *Rationing Health Care*, 90-346 EPW.

Congressional Research Service (1990c), *Health Care Costs at the End of Life*, 90-368 EPW.

Congressional Research Service (1990d), *Taxation of Employer-Provided Health Benefits*, 90-507 EPW.

Congressional Research Service (1991), *National Health Expenditures: Trends from 1960-1989*, 91-588 EPW.

Congressional Research Service (1992a), *Tax Expenditures for Health Care*, 92-12 E.

Congressional Research Service (1992b), *Health Insurance*, IB91093.

Day, P. and R. Klein (1991), "Britain's Health Care Experiment", *Health Affairs*, Fall, pp. 39-59.

Eisenberg, J.M. (forthcoming), "Access to Care and the Challenge of the Uninsured", *Journal of the American Medical Association,* "Contempo 1992" issue.

Englander, A.S. and T. Egebo (1992), "Institutional Commitments and Policy Credibility: A Critical Survey and Evidence from the ERM", *OECD Economic Studies* No. 18, Spring, pp. 45-84.

Englander, A.S. and A. Mittelstädt (1988), "Total Factor Productivity and Structural Aspects of the Slowdown", *OECD Economic Studies* No. 10, Spring, pp. 7-56.

Enthoven, A.C. (1980), *Health Plan*, Addison-Wesley, Reading, Massachusetts.

Enthoven, A.C. (1988), *Theory and Practice of Managed Competition in Health Care Finance*, Elsevier, Amsterdam.

Federal Reserve Board (1992), "Changes in Family Finances from 1983 to 1989: Evidence from the Survey of Consumer Finances", *Federal Reserve Bulletin*, 78, January, pp. 1-18.

Ford, R. and P. Poret (1991), "Infrastructure and Private-Sector Productivity", *OECD Economic Studies* No. 17, Autumn, pp. 63-89.

General Accounting Office (1991a), *Health Insurance Coverage*, GAO/HRD-92-31FS.

General Accounting Office (1991b), *Canadian Health Insurance*, GAO/HRD-91-90.

General Accounting Office (1991c), *US Health Care Spending*, GAO/HRD-91-102.

General Accounting Office (1991d), *Health Care Spending Control*, GAO/HRD-92-9.

General Accounting Office (1992), *Health Care Spending: Nonpolicy Factors Account for Most State Differences*, GAO/HRD-92-36.

Graig, L.A. (1991), *Health of Nations: An International Perspective on US Health Care Reform*, The Wyatt Company, Washington, D.C.

Hufbauer, G.C. and J.J. Schott (1992), *North American Free Trade: Issues and Recommendations*, Institute of International Economics, Washington, D.C.

Jorgenson, D.W. and B.M. Fraumeni (1991), "Investment in Education and U.S. Economic Growth", Harvard Institute of Economic Research Discussion Paper No. 1573.

Ikegami, N. (1991), "Japanese Health Care: Low Cost through Regulated Fees", *Health Affairs,* Fall, pp. 87-109.

Levit, K.R., H.C. Lazenby, C.A. Cowan and S.W. Letsch, "National Health Expenditures, 1990", *Health Care Financing,* Vol. 13, No. 1, Fall, pp. 29-54.

Lewin, L.S., T.J. Eckels and L.B. Miller (1988), "Setting the Record Straight: The Provision of Uncompensated Care by Not-for-profit Hospitals", *New England Journal of Medicine,* May 5, Vol. 318, No. 18, pp. 1212-1215.

Lubitz, J. and R. Prihoda (1984), "The Use and Costs of Medicare Services in the Last 2 years of Life", *Health Care Financing Review,* Vol. 5, No. 3, pp. 117-131.

Lurie, N., N.B. Ward, M.F. Shapiro and R.H. Brook (1984), "Termination from Medi-Cal – Does It Affect Health?", *New England Journal of Medicine,* August 16, Vol. 311, No. 7, pp. 480-484.

Manning, W.G., J.P. Newhouse, N. Duan, E.B. Keeler, A. Leibowitz and M.S. Marquis (1987), "Health Insurance and the Demand for Medical Care: Evidence from a Randomized Experiment", *American Economic Review,* Vol. 77, No. 3, pp. 251-277.

McPherson, K. (1990), "International Differences in Medical Care Practices", *Health Care Systems in Transition,* OECD, Paris; also published as *Health Care Financing: 1989 Annual Supplement,* Department of Health and Human Services, Baltimore.

Naylor, C.D. (1991), "A Different View of Queues in Ontario", *Health Affairs,* Fall, pp. 110-128.

Nicoletti, G. (1988), "A Cross-Country Analysis of Private Consumption, Inflation and the 'Debt Neutrality Hypothesis'", *OECD Economic Studies* No. 11, Autumn, pp. 43-87.

OECD (1987), *Financing and Delivering Health Care: A Comparative Analysis of OECD Countries,* Paris.

OECD (1992), *Progress on Structural Reform,* Paris.

OECD (forthcoming), *The Reform of Health Care: A Comparative Analysis of Seven Countries,* Paris.

Shiels, J., G. Young and R. Ruben (1992), "O Canada: Do we expect too much from its health system?", *Health Affairs,* Spring, pp. 7-20.

Sonnefeld, S.T., D. Waldo, J.A. Lemieux and D.R. McKusick (1991), "Projections of National Health Expenditures through the Year 2000", *Health Care Financing,* Vol. 13, No. 1, Fall, pp. 1-27.

Trajtenberg, M. (1989), "The Welfare Analysis of Product Innovations, with an Application to Computed Tomography Scanners", *Journal of Political Economy,* Vol. 97, No. 2, April, pp. 444-479.

Triplett, J.E. (1992), "Economic Theory and BEA's Alternative Quantity and Price Indexes", *Survey of Current Business,* 72, April, pp. 49-52.

Warshawsky, M.J. (1991a), "Projections of health-care expenditures as a share of GNP: actuarial and economic approaches", Board of Governors of the Federal Reserve System, Finance and Economics Discussion series No. 170, October.

Warshawsky, M.J. (1991*b*), ''Factors contributing to rapid growth in national expenditures on health care'', Board of Governors of the Federal Reserve System, Finance and Economics Discussion Series No. 182, December.

Weisbrod, B.A. (1991), ''The Health Care Quadrilemma: An Essay on Technological Change, Insurance, Quality of Care, and Cost Containment'', *Journal of Economic Literature,* Vol. XXIX, pp. 523-552.

Wenneker, M.B., J.S. Weissman and A.M. Epstein (1990), ''The Association of Payer with Utilisation of Cardiac Procedures in Massachusetts'', *Journal of the American Medical Association,* September 12, Vol. 264, No. 8, pp. 1255-1260.

Wonnacott, R.J. (1991), *The Economics of Overlapping Free Trade Areas and the Mexican Challenge,* C.D. Howe Institute and National Planning Association, Toronto and Washington.

Woolhander, S. and D. Himmelstein (1991), ''The Deteriorating Administrative Efficiency of the U.S. Health Care System'', *New England Journal of Medicine,* Vol. 324, No. 18, May 2, pp. 1253-1258.

Annex I

Calculating the natural unemployment rate and the sacrifice ratio

The natural rate of unemployment and the sacrifice ratio are defined by the relation

$$\Delta p_{t+n} - \Delta p_t = \Sigma_{(i=1,n)} \sigma^{-1}(NR_{t+i} - UN_{t+i}), \ \sigma > 0,$$

where Δp_t is (core) inflation, UN_t is the unemployment rate, NR_t is the natural rate of unemployment, and σ is the sacrifice ratio. The equation says that when the unemployment rate is above the natural rate, inflation will fall. The equation also says that to reduce inflation by one percentage point requires unemployment above the natural rate by σ percentage points for one year.

From 1987 to 1990, the consumer price inflation (CPI) excluding food and energy rose from $4\frac{1}{4}$ per cent to $5\frac{1}{4}$ per cent (all inflation rates are twelve-month changes to the end of the period indicated). However, some of the increase in prices in 1990 was the result of the pass-through of temporarily higher oil costs to non-energy prices. Over the same period, the increase in the employment cost index for wages and salaries (ECI) rose from $3\frac{1}{4}$ per cent in 1987 to 4 per cent in 1990. On balance, underlying inflation probably picked up about $\frac{3}{4}$ percentage point from 1987 to 1990. Over the three years from 1988 to 1990, unemployment averaged 5.4 per cent, so that the natural rate of unemployment was likely above $5\frac{1}{2}$ per cent over this period.

From 1990 to mid-1992, the CPI excluding food and energy has decelerated from a $5\frac{1}{4}$ per cent increase to $3\frac{3}{4}$ per cent, a total of $1\frac{1}{2}$ percentage points. However, since the acceleration calculation discounted about $\frac{1}{4}$ percentage point on account of the oil shock, the deceleration should also, leaving a $1\frac{1}{4}$ percentage point deceleration. Over this period, the ECI has decelerated about $\frac{3}{4}$ percentage point, to $3\frac{1}{4}$ per cent on the latest reading. On balance, there has been a deceleration of about 1 percentage point over this one-and-a-half year period, and the natural rate is likely below the 6.9 per cent average unemployment rate over this period.

A more precise calculation of the natural rate can be made, and an estimate of the sacrifice ratio found, using the equation above. Substituting in the periods of acceleration and deceleration gives a system of two equations in two unknowns:

1987 to 1990: $3/4 = 3 \ \sigma^{-1}(NR - 5.4)$

1990 to mid-1992: $-1 = 1.5 \ \sigma^{-1}(NR - 6.9)$

Solving these two equations gives a natural rate of 5.8 and a sacrifice ratio of 1.6. These values are roughly consistent with conventional wisdom before the recent slowdown

141

began, suggesting that inflation progress in the recent period has been about normal. It should be noted that these are very rough calculations, based on a single episode, and so are potentially not very robust.

Annex II

An overview of health-care financing in selected OECD countries

This annex briefly describes the health-care financing systems in the United States, Japan, Germany, France, the United Kingdom and Canada. The Italian system is described in detail in the forthcoming OECD Economic Survey of Italy. These systems vary widely, but, except for the United States, have the following features in common:

   i) enrolment in a health-care plan is mostly automatic; often, but not always, enrolment is through the workplace;
   ii) insurers of basic health care costs are public or quasi-public; typically they cannot refuse cover;
   iii) there are provisions for those not currently attached to the labour force;
   iv) financing is predominantly through the tax system (often payroll taxes) rather than premiums per enrollee;
   v) patients face virtually no restriction on the choice of physician, and typically little restriction on the choice of hospital;
   vi) the government controls either global expenditure or large components of it (such as physicians' incomes or hospital expenditures).

Although the system in the United States shares some of these features as well, it relies much more heavily on voluntary insurance, usually purchased by employers on behalf of their employees from private, for-profit insurance companies. This system of private insurance is supplemented by large government programmes aimed at the elderly and at some of the poor.

It is traditional to use the language of insurance in describing health-care payment systems, in part because they perform an insurance function by pooling the risk getting ill and incurring medical expenditures. However, except in the United States, there is typically little discretion in either the "purchase" or the "sale" of basic health "insurance" and health-care financing systems therefore resemble government tax-transfer programmes rather than insurance markets.

Material for countries other than the United States is drawn from the far more detailed discussions found in OECD (forthcoming), Congressional Budget Office (1991a), Day and Klein (1991), General Accounting Office (1991b and 1991d), Graig (1991), Ikegami (1991) and OECD (1987).

The United States

Health care is delivered through private insurance, which covers about ¾ of the population; public programmes, which cover more than ¼ of the population; and ad hoc arrangements for the ¹/₇ of the population that has no health insurance coverage. (Because some people are covered under more than one scheme, these figures sum to more than one.) About 80 per cent of those covered through private insurance are enrolled in employer-based group insurance plans, with the rest being covered by individual insurance policies. Employers typically purchase a group policy from one of a large number of private insurance companies, although more recently some, mostly large, employers have chosen instead to pay medical claims as they arise, a practice known as ''self-insurance''. This allows firms to reduce costs and, because employer-run benefit plans (such as pension plans, but also medical benefit plans) are federally regulated under the 1974 Employee Retired Income and Security Act, to avoid state insurance regulations. Many employers, especially smaller ones, do not ensure their employees at all; indeed, a majority of those with no insurance cover are employed or have a family member who is employed.

The two major government health-care payment programmes are Medicare, which essentially covers the old, and Medicaid, which covers some of the poor and offers some financing of long-term care. Governments also support health care through programmes serving military and veterans, public health programmes and public hospitals, whose emergency rooms often provide acute care for some of the uninsured.

Medicare, which was introduced in 1965, is by far the largest government insurance programme. It covers almost everyone over 65 years of age, about 13 per cent of the population, as well as people with certain disabilities (notably, kidney failure), another 1.3 per cent of the population. Hospital expenses under Medicare are funded by a payroll tax. Three-quarters of other expenses (Part B) are funded by general federal government revenues, with premiums, paid by beneficiaries, covering the other quarter. In addition, Medicare patients pay deductibles and co-payments (a payment per service or percentage of the cost of the service, the latter also being referred to as co-insurance). Since Medicare pays for less than half the medical expenses of its beneficiaries, some 70 per cent purchase private supplementary insurance.

The other major government health programme is Medicaid, also established in 1965, which covers mothers with dependent children (68 per cent of Medicaid recipients), the poor elderly (13 per cent), the blind and disabled (15 per cent), and a small number of others. About half of those below the federal poverty line are not covered by Medicaid: single adults below 65 years of age and who are not disabled, are not covered regardless of their income; and people with assets above certain state-defined levels are not eligible. Unlike Medicare, Medicaid covers long-term nursing home care – 40 per cent of the Medicaid expenditures go to nursing home care – for the old and disabled. Medicaid is administered by the states under federal government supervision and guidelines, which govern such things as the type of services provided and the payment schedules for hospitals and physicians. The federal government shares the cost of the programme through grants to the states which depend on state Medicaid expenditures and state personal income levels.

There are more than 575 000 active physicians in the United States, or 2.3 per 1 000 population. A third of them are primary-care physicians and the rest are specialists. By way of comparison, Canada has roughly the same number of physicians per capita, but only half of them are specialists. Physicians are paid predominantly on a fee-for-service basis. Many, however, are paid a salary by a co-ordinated-care, or managed-care, organisation. The oldest form of co-ordinated care is the health maintenance organisation (HMO), in which about $1/7$ of the population is now enrolled. The traditional HMO, exemplified by the large Kaiser Permanente organisation in California, pays health-care providers on a salary and runs its own hospitals and other facilities. Enrollees (or members) receive all their health care from the providers hired by the HMO – that is, the choice of provider is limited. The administrators of the HMO attempt to optimise the health care provided by reviewing medical practice and utilisation, in order to save costs by eliminating unnecessary procedures. More recently, much looser managed-care structures have developed, consisting of affiliations of physicians, who may be paid fee-for-service, rather than a salary. The preferred provider organisation (PPO), a recent development which is similar to a loosely organised HMO, consists of a network of physicians under contract (to an insurance company, for example) to provide care, usually on a fee-for-service basis, but at a discount. Like an HMO, the choice of health-care provider is typically limited to those under contract to the PPO, and these providers are subject to utilisation reviews. A point-of-service (POS) network extends HMOs by allowing patients to choose a non-HMO physician, but only if they pay an extra fee. The POS is an attempt to attract patients who are concerned about the restrictions on physician choice imposed by traditional HMOs.

Japan

Health insurance is universal in Japan, with nearly $2/3$ of the population being covered by mandatory employer plans, and the rest (the retired and the unemployed) by the government-run National Health Insurance (NHI). Firms are required to provide insurance to employees and their dependents, and employees are required to enrol. While there are a large number of insurers, they are highly regulated and neither firms nor employees have a choice of which one to join. Employees of large firms (about $1/4$ of the population) are covered by one of about 1 800 health insurance societies, employees of smaller firms (slightly more than $1/4$) are usually enrolled in a scheme run by the national government, and civil servants and teachers (about 1/10) are covered by one of 82 mutual-aid societies. Taking NHI and small-employer insurance together, the government directly manages the coverage of over 60 per cent of the population. All insurers must provide a legislated basket of services.

Insurance is financed mostly through mandatory payroll taxes, with tax rates that average about 8 per cent, but vary from $3^{1}/2$ to over 13 per cent, depending on the insurer. Employers pay at least half the tax. However, governments pay most administrative costs and subsidise (up to 52 per cent) some insurers from general revenues. Although there are no deductibles, co-payments and co-insurance range from 10 to 30 per cent of the cost of the service, with a monthly cap of about $450.

Hospitals range from prestigious and publicly-owned teaching hospitals to numerous small private clinics (which are typically owned and run by private-practice physicians). About 80 per cent of hospitals and about 94 per cent of clinics are privately owned and operated. Most are owned by physicians and, by law, the chief executive of a hospital must be a physician. Aside from a recent regional ceilings on the number of beds, the government imposes few restrictions on overall hospital expenditures.

About a third of physicians are in private practice and have no access to hospitals, 40 per cent are in non-teaching hospitals and the rest are in teaching hospitals. Primary-care physicians are paid on a fee-for-service basis according to a national rate schedule set by the central government, in consultation with providers and payers. The schedule assigns relative value points for services, which are then translated into monetary terms. Physicians bill the insurers directly and cannot charge their patients extra (balance bill). The government sets targets for total health spending and enforces price control through the fee schedule, but has no formal mechanism to enforce quantity targets on physician services.

Germany

Before unification, West and East Germany had markedly different health systems; this overview discusses only the former. Insurance coverage is essentially complete, except for a small number of people, all of them financially well-off, who choose not to be insured. About $^4/_5$ of the population is covered by the "statutory" scheme, which is administered by some 1 100 sickness funds, which are autonomous from, but highly regulated by, the government. The largest group of sickness funds is organised on a geographical basis, while others are organised on an occupational or enterprise basis. Membership in the statutory scheme is compulsory for several groups, such as workers with incomes below a certain threshold and state pensioners. Retirees are generally covered by the sickness fund to which they belonged when they last worked. About 85 per cent of sickness-fund members are compulsory members, with the rest being voluntary members. Only about half of sickness-fund members, mostly white-collar workers, can choose which fund to belong to. Most of those who are not members of sickness funds are covered by private insurance, although a few members also purchase supplementary private insurance. Several companies, most of them non-profit, offer private insurance, subject to government regulation. A small number of people (members of the armed forces and some people on social welfare) receive free medical care.

The sickness funds are financed by payroll taxes (called "contributions"), shared equally by employer and employee. While the tax rate averages about 13 per cent of wages nation-wide, it varies between 8 and 16 per cent, depending on the fund. Medical services for those who are not covered by sickness funds or private insurance coverage are paid for by the social security fund or from general government revenue. Both sickness funds and private insurers are required by law to provide a certain basket of benefits, although both can offer additional benefits as well.

Primary-care physicians are paid mostly on a fee-for-service basis by the sickness funds. Each fund, in effect, negotiates a lump-sum payment with regional physicians' associations (which are not trade unions), which then divide the money among physicians according to a fee schedule. As a result, within any year the total income of physicians is capped in advance. The associations are responsible for assuring physician quality and quantity control. The fee schedule is negotiated nationally, with each of some 2 500 procedures assigned a relative point value, which is then translated into money by a formula that varies by region, by sickness fund and, to respect the annual cap, by the number of procedures billed. Private insurers must use the same relative point values, but generally have fee scales that are about twice those of the sickness funds.

The hospital system is dominated by public hospitals (half the beds) and private non-profit hospitals ($1/3$ of the beds). The rest are private for-profit hospitals, often owned by physicians. Physicians in public and non-profit hospitals, including most specialists, are paid on salary. Hospital doctors rarely see patients on an out-patient basis, and ambulatory-care doctors rarely have hospital admitting rights. The operating costs of hospitals are paid mostly from the sickness funds and private insurers, while capital expenditures are paid mainly by *Länder* governments, even in for-profit hospitals. As is the case with ambulatory physicians, the sickness funds negotiate an annual lump-sum payment with the hospitals, except that hospitals carry losses or surpluses from one year to the next.

France

Virtually everyone is covered by a statutory health-insurance scheme, which is part of the public social security system. One sickness fund covers most employees and their dependents, or about $4/5$ of the population. Several smaller funds cover the self-employed, farmers and some special groups of workers (miners, for example); these funds also cover retirees. There is also a programme to cover those with no labour force attachment, or about 5 per cent of the population. The sickness funds are quasi-autonomous non-governmental bodies which are managed by employer associations and trade unions, but are subject to close central government regulation, particularly with regard to payroll tax rates and fee schedules. Since the sickness funds require co-payments averaging about 20 per cent and some physicians are allowed to charge patients in excess of the fee schedule, there is a market for supplementary insurance which is provided by several thousand "mutuelles". Although about $4/5$ of the population is covered by supplementary insurance, the market is relatively small: the sickness funds account for over 70 per cent of medical care expenditures and the mutuelles only 6 per cent.

The sickness funds are funded by payroll taxes on employment income (called "contributions"). The tax rates for the large employee sickness fund were 12.6 per cent for the employer and 6.8 per cent for the employee in 1991. The self-employed pay the entire tax on their declared income and pensioners pay a 1 per cent tax on their pension income. Sickness funds cover medical and pharmaceutical expenditures according to national schedules. There are substantial co-payments for physicians and drugs – 25 and between 30 and 60 per cent of the schedules – but low co-payments for hospital care. The mutuelles sell insurance based on actuarial risk and benefits.

About $2/3$ of physicians are paid on a fee-for-service basis by their patients, who are then (partially) reimbursed by their sickness funds and mutuelles. Almost all of these physicians are members of the statutory scheme, but there are two types of membership: a doctor can charge no more than the fee schedule and receives a pension and national health insurance for free; or, a doctor can charge more than the schedule but must pay for the pension and insurance. About ¼ of physicians have opted for the second type of membership, mainly specialists and those practising in large cities. The fee schedule, which is set by the national government, comprises a relative value scale of some 4 000 procedures. Apart from this schedule, however, neither the government nor the sickness funds have much control over fee-for-service physicians' incomes. The other ⅓ of physicians are salaried employees of the government, who work mainly in public hospitals.

Public hospitals account for about ⅔ of beds and are staffed largely by full-time and part-time salaried physicians. Private, for-profit hospitals and clinics account for the remainder of the beds, and these are staffed by fee-for-service physicians. Public hospitals tend to be large, general facilities, while private hospitals tend to be small and to specialise in services such as obstetrics, certain types of elective surgery and long-term care. As is the case with physicians, the hospital is paid by the patient, who is then reimbursed, although it is customary for the sickness funds to meet in-patient expenses directly (except perhaps for small co-payments).

United Kingdom

The health-care system has recently undergone a transformation as the result of reforms introduced from 1989 to 1991. These reforms are generally designed to increase the responsiveness of the system by introducing a form of managed competition, especially in the hospital sector.

Everyone is eligible to receive mostly free medical care through the National Health Service (NHS), which accounts for about 88 per cent of total health expenditures. Patients register with a general practitioner (GP), who provides primary care and referrals to specialists. Until recently, the choice was officially unrestricted but, in practice, it was often difficult to change one's GP. One result of the recent reforms is that the district health authorities are to provide service through contracts with doctors and hospitals, which may lead to restrictions on choice. In addition to the NHS, there is a small, but growing, private-care sector, which generally features less queuing for elective procedures. About 1/10 of the population is covered by private insurance, which typically restricts coverage to acute, non-emergency hospital care and specialist physician services.

General tax revenues provide about 80 per cent of NHS funding, a payroll tax ("national insurance contribution") another 15 per cent, and various charges the remaining 5 per cent. Private expenditure, accounting for the 12 per cent of total health expenditure not covered by the NHS, pays mostly for direct purchases (of drugs, for example), with about ⅓ of it going to private health insurance. Private insurance is sold mainly by competing non-profit insurers, typically requires deductibles or co-payments and has premiums based on assessed risk. Private insurers can refuse coverage or refuse to cover pre-existing medical conditions.

Just over ⅓ of physicians are GPs, who work as independent contractors to the NHS. Just under half their income is in the form of a lump sum, or capitation, for each patient registered in a practice (the capitation varies with the age of the patient). Fees for some services (for instance, immunisation) and an allowance for actual practice expenses (such as office rent) and other allowances account for the rest of GPs' incomes. It is common for GPs to form group practices, in order to share secretarial services, for example. Average payments to all GPs are set by the government based on the recommendation of an independent body. If physicians provide services in excess of what is forecast, fees and allowances are reduced to compensate. However, if their costs rise, fees and allowances are raised to cover actual costs. Physicians on hospital staffs are salaried (but many also work in private practice) and those in the private sector bill on a fee-for-service basis.

Before April 1991, hospitals were run by district health authorities and received global lump-sum budgets, set ultimately by the central government. The reforms separated the function of payer of hospital services from that of provider. The district health authorities remain as the major payer, although large group practices of GPs also have a role. They will receive a capitation payment from the government and will then contract with hospitals for the provision of services. Well-managed NHS hospitals are to have the option of becoming self-governing "trusts" and to compete with other institutions (private hospitals, for example) for contracts from district health authorities and GPs. It is hoped that the competition engendered by this arrangement will increase both the efficiency and responsiveness of hospital-care delivery, while the principle of capitation payments from the government contains overall costs.

Canada

Universal health insurance coverage is provided through provincial health care plans in which "enrolment" is automatic and free. The plans place no restrictions on which physicians or hospitals a person may use, although procedures done outside the province may not be fully reimbursed, if the costs exceed the fee schedules of the patient's home province. In return for partial federal funding, provinces must agree to certain terms in the provision of health care funding, such as universal coverage, free access and a basket of minimum services. As the plans do not cover all procedures – dental services, prescription drugs and private hospital rooms, for example, are generally not covered – many people purchase supplementary insurance, often through their employer.

The public system is funded partly from provincial general revenues or payroll taxes and partly from federal general revenues. There are no deductibles, co-payments or co-insurance for physician or hospital services covered by the provincial plans, although private insurance policies may have these features. Physicians who have joined the provincial plans bill them directly, and cannot bill any additional amount to patients.

Physicians are paid on a fee-for-service basis, and for procedures covered by the government plan, exclusively by the provincial government. Although physicians are not required to join the government plan, anyone who "opts out" cannot bill any procedures through the plan; therefore, very few have opted out. Thus, for the bulk of medical procedures, there is only one payer. The fee schedule is set by the provincial government, in practice with the participation of physician groups. Some provincial governments set a total annual budget as well, implying that increases in the number of procedures, for instance, must be offset by a reductions in the average payment per procedure.

149

Hospitals are almost entirely either public (including those attached to universities, which are themselves public) or non-profit community facilities. They receive about ⁴/₅ of their budgets from provincial governments, largely in the form of lump-sum grants. Other sources of funds are charitable donations, fees charged for private rooms and miscellaneous fees (such as parking fees); deductibles and co-payments are not permitted. The provincial governments attempt to shape the hospital system by controlling the number of beds funded and capital expenditure (for example, the construction of a cardiac unit). However, hospital administrators are generally responsible for allocating the provincial lump sum grants within the hospital.

STATISTICAL AND STRUCTURAL ANNEX

Selected background statistics

	Average 1982-91	1982	1983	1984	1985	1986	1987	1988	1989	1990	1991
A. Percentage change from previous year at constant 1987 prices											
Private consumption	2.7	1.1	4.6	4.8	4.4	3.6	2.8	3.6	1.9	1.2	-0.6
Gross fixed capital formation	1.2	-8.0	6.6	15.9	5.0	0.4	-0.5	4.2	0.4	-3.1	-8.5
Residential	2.3	-18.1	40.4	14.4	1.3	12.0	-0.4	-1.1	-3.8	-9.1	-12.6
Non-residential	1.2	-4.6	-3.0	16.5	6.4	-4.1	-0.5	6.6	2.2	-0.8	-7.1
GDP	2.3	-2.2	3.9	6.2	3.2	2.9	3.1	3.9	2.5	0.8	-1.2
GDP price deflator	4.1	6.2	4.1	4.5	3.6	2.7	3.2	3.9	4.4	4.4	4.0
Industrial production	2.3	-4.4	3.6	9.4	1.7	1.0	4.9	5.4	2.6	1.0	-1.9
Employment	1.5	-0.9	1.3	4.1	2.0	2.3	2.6	2.3	2.0	0.5	-0.9
Compensation of employees (current prices)	6.5	5.5	5.9	9.7	7.0	5.9	6.9	8.3	6.2	6.1	3.0
Productivity (GDP/employment)	0.7	-0.9	3.3	1.8	0.5	1.2	0.3	0.8	0.0	-0.4	0.0
Unit labour costs (compensation/GDP)	4.1	7.9	2.0	3.3	3.7	2.9	3.7	4.2	3.6	5.2	4.2
B. Percentage ratios											
Gross fixed capital formation as per cent of GDP at constant prices	15.7	14.8	15.2	16.6	16.9	16.5	15.9	16.0	15.6	15.0	13.9
Stockbuilding as per cent of GDP at constant prices	0.4	-0.5	0.1	1.6	0.5	0.2	0.6	0.4	0.7	0.1	-0.2
Foreign balance as per cent of GDP at constant prices	-2.0	-0.2	-1.4	-2.9	-3.4	-3.5	-3.1	-2.2	-1.6	-1.1	-0.5
Compensation of employees as per cent of GDP at current prices	59.5	60.8	59.6	59.0	59.0	59.1	59.4	59.6	59.1	59.6	59.7
Direct taxes as per cent of household income	12.1	12.8	11.9	11.6	12.0	11.8	12.5	11.9	12.5	12.3	11.8
Household saving as per cent of disposable income	6.0	8.9	6.9	8.3	6.6	6.2	4.5	4.5	4.5	4.5	4.9
Unemployment as per cent of total labour force	7.0	9.7	9.6	7.5	7.2	7.0	6.2	5.5	5.3	5.5	6.7
C. Other indicator											
Current balance (billion dollars)	-90.9	-11.4	-43.6	-98.8	-121.7	-147.5	-163.5	-126.7	-101.1	-90.4	-3.7

Sources: US Department of Commerce, Survey of Current Business, and OECD.

Table A. National product and expenditure
Seasonally adjusted, percentage changes from previous period, annual rates, 1987 prices

	Average 1981-91	1981	1982	1983	1984	1985	1986	1987	1988	1989	1990	1991
Private consumption	2.6	1.2	1.1	4.6	4.8	4.4	3.6	2.8	3.6	1.9	1.2	-0.6
Public expenditure	2.7	1.3	1.5	2.8	3.1	6.1	5.2	3.0	0.6	1.5	3.3	1.2
Gross fixed investment	1.2	0.6	-8.0	6.6	15.9	5.0	0.4	-0.5	4.2	0.4	-3.1	-8.5
Residential	1.4	-8.1	-18.1	40.4	14.4	1.3	12.0	-0.4	-1.1	-3.8	-9.1	-12.6
Non-residential	1.4	3.9	-4.6	-3.0	16.5	6.4	-4.1	-0.5	6.6	2.2	-0.8	-7.1
Final domestic demand	2.4	1.1	-0.3	4.6	6.2	4.8	3.4	2.3	3.1	1.6	0.9	-1.4
Stockbuilding[1]	0.0	0.9	-1.1	0.6	1.6	-1.1	-0.3	0.4	-0.1	0.3	-0.5	-0.3
Total domestic demand	2.4	2.0	-1.4	5.2	7.8	3.6	3.0	2.7	3.0	1.9	0.3	-1.8
Exports of goods and services	5.1	1.7	-9.0	-3.6	6.9	1.2	6.6	10.5	15.8	11.3	8.7	5.8
Imports of goods and services	6.4	4.9	-0.0	12.5	25.0	6.3	6.6	4.6	3.7	3.7	3.1	-0.1
Foreign balance[1]	-0.2	-0.2	-0.8	-1.3	-1.7	-0.6	-0.2	0.3	0.9	0.6	0.5	0.6
GDP	2.3	1.8	-2.2	3.9	6.2	3.2	2.9	3.1	3.9	2.5	0.8	-1.2

	1991 levels (1987 $ billions)	1989 Q4	1990 Q1	1990 Q2	1990 Q3	1990 Q4	1991 Q1	1991 Q2	1991 Q3	1991 Q4	1992 Q1	1992 Q2
Private consumption	3 240.8	0.1	2.2	0.7	1.7	-3.1	-3.0	2.0	1.5	-0.3	5.1	-0.1
Public expenditure	941.0	0.7	8.1	1.1	-2.0	6.1	2.8	0.2	-2.3	-3.0	1.7	-1.2
Gross fixed investment	670.4	-3.9	3.4	-9.2	-2.9	-13.1	-18.7	-0.7	0.8	-1.1	7.4	15.2
Residential	170.2	-7.3	5.5	-15.9	-22.9	-22.4	-26.9	7.0	14.4	11.3	20.1	12.6
Non-residential	500.2	-2.5	2.6	-6.6	5.6	-9.6	-15.8	-3.1	-3.4	-5.2	3.0	16.1
Final domestic demand	4 852.2	-0.4	3.5	-1.2	0.3	-3.0	-4.3	1.3	0.6	-0.9	4.7	1.7
Stockbuilding[1]	-9.4	0.2	-0.5	0.5	-0.4	-0.8	0.0	0.1	0.4	0.1	-0.4	0.4
Total domestic demand	4 842.8	0.4	1.6	0.8	-1.4	-6.0	-4.2	1.7	2.4	-0.4	3.0	3.4
Exports of goods and services	539.4	13.7	12.4	7.0	-0.2	11.6	-5.0	16.6	6.2	13.3	2.9	-1.4
Imports of goods and services	561.2	4.0	2.1	5.1	1.5	-8.5	-14.6	15.6	17.1	4.2	3.5	14.7
Foreign balance[1]	-21.8	0.2	0.2	0.0	-0.0	0.5	0.3	0.0	-0.3	0.2	-0.0	-0.5
GDP	4 821.0	1.2	2.6	1.0	-1.6	-3.9	-3.0	1.7	1.2	0.6	2.9	1.5

1. Changes as a percentage of previous period GDP.
Source: US Department of Commerce, Survey of Current Business.

Table B. Labour Market (s.a.)

	1983	1984	1985	1986	1987	1988	1989	1990	1991	Q2	1991 Q3	Q4	1992 Q1	Q2
1. Number of persons, millions														
Population of working age[1,2]	174.2	176.4	178.2	180.6	182.8	184.6	186.4	188.0	189.8	189.5	190.0	190.4	190.9	191.3
Civilian labour force[1]	111.5	113.5	115.5	117.8	119.9	121.7	123.9	124.8	125.3	125.5	125.3	125.5	126.3	127.2
Unemployment[1]	10.7	8.5	8.3	8.2	7.4	6.7	6.5	6.9	8.4	8.5	8.5	8.7	9.1	9.5
Employment[1]	100.8	105.0	107.2	109.6	112.4	115.0	117.3	117.9	116.9	117.0	116.8	116.8	117.2	117.6
Employment[3]	90.2	94.5	97.5	99.5	102.2	105.5	108.1	110.0	108.3	108.2	108.3	108.2	108.1	108.4
Federal government	2.8	2.8	2.9	2.9	2.9	3.0	3.0	3.1	3.0	3.0	3.0	3.0	3.0	3.0
State and local	13.1	13.2	13.5	13.8	14.1	14.4	14.8	15.2	15.4	15.4	15.4	15.4	15.5	15.6
Manufacturing	18.4	19.4	19.3	19.0	19.0	19.3	19.4	19.1	18.5	18.4	18.4	18.4	18.3	18.3
Construction	3.9	4.4	4.7	4.8	5.0	5.1	5.2	5.1	4.7	4.7	4.7	4.6	4.6	4.6
Other	51.9	54.7	57.2	59.0	61.2	63.7	65.9	67.4	67.4	66.7	66.8	66.8	66.8	67.0
2. Percentage change from previous period (s.a.a.r.)														
Population of working age[1,2]	1.1	1.2	1.0	1.3	1.2	1.0	1.0	0.9	0.9	0.9	1.0	1.0	0.9	0.9
Civilian labour force	1.2	1.8	1.7	2.1	1.7	1.5	1.8	0.8	0.4	1.5	-0.7	0.8	2.6	2.8
Employment[1]	1.3	4.1	2.0	2.3	2.6	2.3	2.0	0.5	-0.9	0.3	-0.8	0.1	1.3	1.6
Employment[3]	0.7	4.8	3.2	2.1	2.7	3.3	2.6	1.3	-1.3	-1.3	0.1	-0.2	-0.2	1.1
Federal government	1.3	1.2	2.4	0.8	1.5	0.9	0.6	3.3	-3.9	1.2	1.4	1.4	0.3	-0.4
State and local government	-0.0	0.9	2.3	2.0	2.0	2.5	2.6	2.9	1.3	1.0	-0.1	0.9	1.2	1.8
Manufacturing	-1.9	5.1	-0.6	-1.5	0.3	1.7	0.5	-1.7	-3.5	-3.0	-0.4	-1.5	-1.6	-0.4
Construction	0.9	11.1	6.7	3.1	3.1	2.9	1.5	-0.9	-8.8	-6.2	-2.8	-5.0	-1.4	1.9
Other	1.8	5.3	4.5	3.3	3.6	4.1	3.5	2.3	-0.6	-1.1	0.4	0.1	-0.0	1.3
3. Unemployment rates														
Total	9.6	7.5	7.2	7.0	6.2	5.5	5.3	5.5	6.7	6.7	6.8	6.9	7.2	7.5
Married men	6.4	4.6	4.3	4.4	3.9	3.2	3.1	3.4	4.4	4.4	4.4	4.5	4.9	5.0
Females	9.2	7.6	7.4	7.1	6.2	5.6	5.4	5.4	6.4	6.3	6.3	6.7	6.7	7.0
Youths	22.4	18.9	18.6	18.4	16.9	15.3	15.0	15.5	18.7	18.7	19.0	19.0	19.6	20.9
4. Activity rate[4]	57.9	59.5	60.1	60.7	61.5	62.3	62.9	62.7	61.6	61.7	61.5	61.3	61.4	61.5

1. Household survey.
2. Non-institutional population aged 16 and over.
3. Non-agricultural payroll.
4. Employment as percentage of population aged from 16 to 64.
Source: Department of Labor, Monthly Labor Review.

Table C. Costs and prices
Percentage changes from previous period, s.a.a.r.

	1983	1984	1985	1986	1987	1988	1989	1990	1991	1991 Q2	1991 Q3	1991 Q4	1992 Q1	1992 Q2
Rates of pay														
Major wage settlements[1]	3.9	3.7	3.2	2.3	3.1	2.6	3.2	3.5	3.5	4.0	4.4	2.8	2.4	4.0
Hourly earnings index[2]	4.4	3.7	3.0	2.3	2.5	3.3	4.0	3.7	3.1	4.0	2.6	2.2	3.1	1.8
Wages and salaries per person	4.8	5.2	4.6	4.1	4.5	4.7	3.3	4.7	3.6	4.1	3.7	2.9	3.3	1.7
Compensation per person	4.6	5.4	4.9	3.6	4.2	5.9	4.0	5.6	3.9	4.1	4.1	3.1	3.7	1.9
Productivity, non-farm business														
Hourly	2.4	2.1	0.8	2.0	0.8	0.9	-1.0	-0.0	0.1	1.1	1.9	2.2	4.1	1.8
Per employee	3.7	3.3	0.1	0.7	1.4	1.1	-0.9	-1.2	-0.9	2.3	1.5	1.8	2.6	0.8
Unit labour cost, non-farm business	1.5	1.9	3.3	2.9	2.6	3.2	4.3	5.3	4.5	4.0	1.8	0.6	0.3	0.6
Prices														
GDP deflator	4.1	4.5	3.6	2.7	3.2	3.9	4.4	4.4	4.0	3.5	2.7	2.3	3.1	2.6
Private consumption deflator	4.8	4.0	3.9	3.1	4.2	4.2	4.7	5.3	4.3	3.3	2.9	3.2	3.1	3.4
Consumer price index	3.2	4.3	3.5	1.9	3.7	4.1	4.8	5.4	4.2	2.4	3.2	3.1	2.8	3.3
Food	2.1	3.9	2.2	3.2	4.2	4.1	5.8	5.8	2.9	4.0	-1.0	1.4	1.1	0.7
Wholesale prices	1.2	2.4	-0.5	-2.9	2.6	4.0	5.0	3.6	0.2	-3.9	-0.6	0.3	-1.1	4.1
Crude products	1.3	2.2	-7.5	-8.4	6.7	2.5	7.4	5.7	-7.0	-18.0	-7.8	0.9	-5.1	11.4
Intermediate products	0.6	2.5	-0.4	-3.5	2.4	5.5	4.6	2.2	-0.0	-4.4	0.7	-1.0	-1.9	3.8
Finished products	1.6	2.1	0.9	-1.4	2.1	2.5	5.1	4.9	2.1	0.2	-0.1	1.9	-0.3	3.2

1. Total effective wage adjustment in all industries under collective agreements in non-farm industry covering at least 1000 workers, not seasonally adjusted.
2. Production or non-supervisory workers on private non-agricultural payrolls.
Sources: Department of Labor, Bureau of Labor Statistics, Monthly Labor Review; US Department of Commerce, Survey of Current Business.

Table E. **Monetary Indicators**

	1983	1984	1985	1986	1987	1988	1989	1990	1991	1991 Q2	1991 Q3	1991 Q4	1992 Q1	1992 Q2
Monetary aggregates (percentage changes from previous period) s.a.a.r														
M1	11.1	7.0	9.1	13.5	11.6	4.2	1.0	3.7	6.0	7.6	7.7	11.5	17.5	10.3
M2	12.5	8.0	9.1	8.2	6.6	5.1	3.8	5.4	3.2	4.5	0.6	2.3	4.4	-0.0
M3	9.9	10.2	8.9	8.4	6.9	6.5	4.3	2.6	1.6	1.8	-1.3	0.9	2.2	-1.8
Velocity of circulation														
GDP / M1	6.8	7.0	6.9	6.4	6.1	6.3	6.7	6.8	6.6	6.7	6.6	6.5	6.3	6.2
GDP / M2	1.6	1.7	1.6	1.6	1.6	1.6	1.7	1.7	1.7	1.7	1.7	1.7	1.7	1.7
GDP / M3	1.3	1.3	1.3	1.3	1.3	1.3	1.3	1.3	1.4	1.4	1.4	1.4	1.4	1.4
Federal Reserve Bank reserves ($ billion)														
Non-borrowed	28.3	27.0	32.9	39.7	45.6	44.9	45.7	47.2	42.7	42.0	42.5	44.7	47.3	49.1
Borrowed	1.9	3.7	1.3	0.8	0.8	2.4	1.1	0.9	0.4	0.3	0.7	0.2	0.1	0.2
Total	30.2	30.7	34.3	40.6	46.3	47.2	46.9	48.1	43.1	42.3	43.2	44.8	47.5	49.2
Required	28.9	30.0	33.5	39.7	45.3	46.2	45.9	47.1	41.9	41.3	42.2	43.9	46.4	48.2
Excess	1.3	0.7	0.8	0.9	1.0	1.0	1.0	1.0	1.2	1.0	1.0	1.0	1.0	1.0
Free (excess − borrowed)	-0.5	-3.1	-0.5	0.1	0.3	-1.3	-0.2	0.0	0.8	0.7	0.3	0.8	0.9	0.8
Interest rates (%)														
Federal funds rate	9.1	10.2	8.1	6.8	6.7	7.6	9.2	8.1	5.7	5.9	5.6	4.8	4.0	3.8
Discount rate[1]	8.5	8.8	7.7	6.3	5.7	6.2	7.0	7.0	5.4	5.7	5.3	4.5	3.5	3.5
Prime rate[2]	10.8	12.0	9.9	8.3	8.2	9.3	10.9	10.0	8.5	8.7	8.3	7.7	6.5	6.5
3 month Treasury Bills	8.6	9.5	7.5	6.0	5.8	6.7	8.1	7.5	5.4	5.6	5.4	4.5	3.9	3.7
AAA rate[3]	12.0	12.7	11.4	9.0	9.4	9.7	9.3	9.3	8.8	8.9	8.8	8.4	8.3	8.3
10 year Treasury Bonds	11.1	12.4	10.6	7.7	8.4	8.8	8.5	8.6	7.9	8.1	7.9	7.3	7.3	7.4

1. Rate for Federal Reserve Bank of New York.
2. Prime rate on short-term business loans.
3. Corporate Bonds, AAA rating group, quoted by Moody's Investors Services.
Source: Board of the Governors of the Federal Reserve System, Federal Reserve Bulletin.

	1978	1979	1980	1981	198
Exports, fob[1]	142 075	184 439	224 250	237 044	211
Imports, fob[1]	176 002	212 007	249 750	265 067	247
Trade balance	–33 927	–27 568	–25 500	–28 023	–36 4
Services, net[2]	24 572	33 876	36 166	44 755	42
Balance on goods and services	–9 355	6 308	10 666	16 732	5
Private transfers, net	–844	–920	–1 044	–4 516	–8
Official transfers, net	–4 944	–5 673	–7 304	–7 186	–8
Current balance	–15 143	–285	2 318	5 030	–11 4
US assets abroad other than official reserves	–61 862	–64 922	–78 813	–108 972	–117
US private assets, net[3]	–57 202	–61 176	–73 651	–103 875	–111
Reported by U.S. banks	–33 667	–26 213	–46 838	–84 175	–111
US government assets[4]	–4 660	–3 746	–5 162	–5 097	–6
Foreign assets in the United States					
Liabilities to foreign official monetary agencies[5]	33 678	–13 665	15 497	4 960	3
Other liabilities to foreign monetary agencies[6]	30 358	52 416	42 615	78 072	88
Reported by U.S. banks	16 141	32 607	10 743	42 128	65
Allocation of SDR's	–	1 139	1 152	1 093	
Errors and omissions	12 236	26 449	25 386	24 992	41
Change in reserves (+ = increase)	–732	1 133	8 155	5 176	4
a) Gold	65	65	–	–	
b) Currency assets	4 683	–257	6 472	861	1
c) Reserve position in IMF	–4 231	189	1 667	2 491	2
d) Special drawing rights	–1 249	1 136	16	1 824	1

1. Excluding military goods.
2. Services include reinvested earnings of incorporated affiliates.
3. Including: Direct investment financed by reinvested earnings of incorporated affiliates; foreign securities; US claims on unaf
   foreigners reported by US nonbanking concerns; and US claims reported by US banks, not included elsewhere.
4. Including: US credits and other long–term assets; repayments on US credits and other long–term assets, US foreign cu
   holdings and US short–term assets, net.
Source: US Department of Commerce, Survey of Current Business.

983	1984	1985	1986	1987	1988	1989	1990	1991
799	219 926	215 915	223 344	250 208	320 230	361 697	388 705	415 962
901	332 418	338 088	368 425	409 765	447 189	477 365	497 558	489 398
102	−112 492	−122 173	−145 081	−159 557	−126 959	−115 668	−108 853	−73 436
221	34 280	23 402	21 728	19 136	25 173	40 132	51 342	61 725
881	−78 212	−98 771	−123 353	−140 421	−101 786	−75 536	−57 511	−11 711
066	−9 756	−9 545	−10 112	−10 544	−11 863	−12 316	−12 374	−12 996
676	−10 855	−13 406	−14 064	−12 508	−13 007	−13 290	−20 542	21 025
623	−98 823	−121 722	−147 529	−163 473	−126 656	−101 142	−90 427	−3 682
660	−26 094	−30 212	−91 382	−71 550	−88 795	−89 651	−54 163	−67 982
654	−20 605	−27 391	−89 360	−72 556	−91 762	−90 922	−56 467	−71 379
928	−11 127	−1 323	−59 975	−42 119	−56 322	−51 255	7 469	−4 753
006	−5 489	−2 821	−2 022	1 006	2 967	1 271	2 304	3 397
845	3 140	−1 119	35 648	45 387	39 759	8 489	33 908	18 407
534	98 870	132 084	187 543	184 585	179 731	205 204	65 471	48 573
342	33 849	41 045	79 783	89 026	70 235	63 382	16 370	−13 678
−	26 038	24 825	15 407	−4 096	−126	2 394	47 370	−1 078
196	3 130	3 858	−313	−9 149	3 912	25 293	2 158	−5 763
−	−	−	−	−	−	−	−	−
304	1 156	3 869	942	−7 588	5 064	25 229	2 697	−6 307
434	995	−908	−1 501	−2 070	−1 025	−471	−731	367
66	979	897	246	509	−127	535	192	177

luding: US Government securities and other US Government liabilities, US liabilities reported by US banks not included ewhere and other foreign official assets.
luding direct investment: US Treasury securities; other US securities; US liabilities to unaffiliated foreigners reported by US n–banking concerns; US liabilities reported by US banks not included elsewhere.

159

Table F. **Public sector**

	1960	1970	1980	1988	1989	1990	1991
A. Budget indicators							
General government accounts (% GDP)							
Current receipts	27.0	29.7	30.5	30.5	30.8	30.9	30.8
Non-interest expenditures	25.0	29.6	30.6	30.5	30.3	31.2	31.9
Primary budget balance	2.0	0.1	–0.1	–0.1	0.5	–0.4	–1.1
Net interest	–1.3	–1.2	–1.2	–1.9	–2.0	–2.1	–2.3
General government budget balance	0.7	–1.1	–1.3	–2.0	–1.6	–2.5	–3.4
of which:							
Central government	0.7	–1.3	–2.2	–2.8	–2.4	–3.0	–3.7
Excluding Social security [1]	–	–	–2.2	–3.8	–3.6	–4.1	–4.4
B. The structure of expenditure and taxation (% GDP)							
Government expenditure							
Transfers	5.7	8.3	11.7	11.6	11.7	12.3	12.7
Subsidies	0.1	0.3	0.2	0.2	0.1	0.1	0.0
General expenditures							
Education	3.5	5.3	5.2	5.1	5.1	5.3	5.4
Transportation	2.0	2.0	1.7	1.5	1.5	1.5	1.5
Health	0.8	2.2	3.1	3.7	3.9	4.2	4.7

	United States			OECD average		
	1988	1989	1990	1988	1989	1990
Tax receipts						
Income tax	10.2	10.6	10.7	11.9	11.4	11.7
Social security tax	8.7	8.6	8.8	9.2	9.2	9.3
Consumption tax	4.3	4.2	4.3	11.4	11.1	11.1

	Prior to Tax Reduction	Under the Tax Reduction
C. Tax rates (%)		
Average rate of income tax [2]	13.0	11.9
Top rate	50.0	28.0
Lower rate	11.0	15.0
Average marginal rate [2]	20.2	18.6
Income tax elasticity [2]	1.55	1.56
Social security tax rate	7.15	7.15
VAT rate	–	–
Corporation tax rate	51.0	45.0
Effective tax rate on corporate investment	33.3	36.5
Equipment	10.0	39.6
Non-residential housing	34.4	43.1
Owner-occupied housing	22.5	23.7

	1960	1970	1980	1988	1989	1990	1991
Income tax as % of total tax	32.7	35.2	36.9	34.8	35.7	35.8	34.8
D. Government debt (% GDP)							
General government gross debt	60.3	45.5	38.1	53.2	54.1	56.4	59.8
Net debt	45.1	27.9	18.7	30.9	30.5	33.1	34.7

1. OECD estimates derived from fiscal year off-budget items (primarily retirement pension balance), converted to a calendar year basis.
2. Federal government.
Sources: Economic Report of the President, February 1991; Department of Treasury, Office of Tax Analysis; Revenue Statistics of OECD Member Countries, 1965-1990, OECD 1991, and OECD calculations.

Table G. Financial markets

	1970	1975	1980	1987	1988	1989	1990	1991
A. Financial and corporate flows								
Share of private financial institutions' financial assets in national net assets (%)[1]	<3.1	40.0	37.3	55.8	57.8	60.3	62.6	67.0
Market value of equities including corporate farm equities (billions of dollars)[1]	0.648	0.684	1.293	2.344	2.577	3.211	3.005	3.688
Debt-to-equities ratio in non-financial corporate business excluding farms (%)[1]	54.3	77.8	64.0	74.5	74.8	65.3	72.2	59.4
Ratio of market value to net worth[1]	50.8	42.8	41.0	58.2	61.0	74.4	70.2	90.5
B. Foreign sector (billions of dollars)								
Net foreign assets outstanding[1,3]	58.3	86.0	259.9	-144.8	-280.9	-374.0	-390.8	-417.1
Changes in net foreign investment[2]	3.0	24.0	31.3	-169.3	-134.8	-87.9	-31.6	34.8
of which net financial investment of:								
Private sectors	15.3	92.0	103.5	39.8	105.5	168.8	168.1	289.3
Public sectors	-22.2	-80.0	-63.7	-186.7	-194.1	-224.7	231.6	-297.0
Foreign purchases of U.S. corporate equities[2]	0.7	4.7	4.2	15.6	-0.5	7.0	-14.7	9.8
U.S. purchases of foreign equities[2]	1.1	-0.9	2.4	-2.1	0.9	17.3	6.9	34.2
C. Net worth (billions of dollars)[1]								
Total, all sectors	3.049	5.526	10.625	14.246	16.950	18.010	18.086	18.385
Private, consolidated	3.435	6.098	11.664	15.944	19.093	20.321	20.566	21.133
Household	3.338	5.109	9.584	13.861	16.930	18.599	18.585	20.101
Total owner-occupied real estate	0.872	1.580	3.306	5.262	5.518	6.954	5.877	6.336
Home mortgages as a per cent of owner-occupied real estate	33.2	29.7	28.5	35.8	38.3	39.4	46.1	45.0
D. Debt to net worth ratios, Private sector (%)[4]								
Household	14.1	14.7	14.9	18.2	18.8	18.8	21.0	20.2
Non-farm non-corporate business	32.9	44.0	43.6	68.3	68.7	62.0	66.3	63.0
Farm business	19.5	17.6	17.9	20.8	18.6	18.7	18.8	19.0
Non-financial corporate business excluding farms	44.0	33.4	26.3	43.4	45.7	48.6	50.7	53.8
Private financial institutions	72.0	87.1	77.2	106.2	105.2	107.8	116.6	108.5

1. Data are year-end outstandings.
2. Data are annual flows.
3. Net foreign assets exclude U.S. residents' holdings of foreign equities and foreign residents' holdings of U.S. equities.
4. Debt is credit market debt.
Source: Balance Sheets for the U.S. Economy, 1945-90.

Table H. Labour market indicators

A. Evolution

	Peak	Trough	1987	1988	1989	1990	1991
Standardised unemployment rate	1982: 9.6	1969: 3.4	6.1	5.4	5.2	5.4	6.7
Unemployment rate							
Total	1982: 9.5	1969: 3.4	6.1	5.4	5.2	5.4	6.6
Male	1983: 9.7	1969: 2.7	6.1	5.3	5.1	5.5	6.9
Female	1982: 9.4	1969: 4.7	6.2	5.6	5.3	5.4	6.3
Youth[1]	1982: 17.0	1969: 7.4	11.7	10.6	10.5	10.7	12.9
Share of long-term unemployment[2]	1983: 13.4	1969: 1.9	8.1	7.4	5.8	5.6	
Productivity index, 1987=100[3]			100.0	101.6	102.1	102.6	102.8

B. Structural or institutional characteristics

		1970	1980	1987	1988	1989	1990	1991
Participation rate[4]								
Global		60.4	63.8	65.6	65.9	66.5	66.4	66.0
Male		79.7	77.4	76.2	76.2	76.4	76.1	75.5
Female		43.3	51.5	56.0	56.6	57.4	57.5	57.3
Employment / population between 16 and 64 years		57.4	59.2	61.5	62.3	63.0	62.7	61.6
Employment by sector								
Agriculture	– per cent of total	4.5	3.6	3.0	2.9	2.9	2.8	2.9
	– per cent change	-3.6	0.6	1.4	-2.1	1.4	-0.6	1.0
Industry	– per cent of total	34.3	30.5	27.1	26.9	26.7	26.2	25.3
	– per cent change	-1.8	-1.9	0.4	1.6	1.1	-1.2	-4.3
Services	– per cent of total	61.1	65.9	69.9	70.2	70.5	71.0	71.8
	– per cent change	3.0	1.7	3.5	2.7	2.4	1.2	0.3
of which: Government	– per cent of total	0.2	0.2	0.2	0.2	0.2	0.2	0.2
	– per cent change	3.0	1.8	1.9	2.2	2.3	3.0	0.4
Voluntary part-time work[5]		13.9	14.2	13.9	13.9	14.0	13.7	13.7
Social insurance as a percent of compensation		10.8	16.3	16.2	16.3	16.6	16.8	17.1
Government unemployment insurance benefits[6]		12.3	12.6	8.1	7.9	8.3	9.3	10.9
Minimum wage: as a percentage of average wage[7]		49.6	46.6	37.3	36.1	34.7	36.8	40.0

1. People between 16 and 24 years as a percentage of the labour force of the same age group.
2. People looking for a job since one year or more as a percentage of total unemployment.
3. Production as a percentage of employment.
4. Labour force as a percentage of the corresponding population aged between 16 and 64 years.
5. As a percentage of salaried workers.
6. Value of the unemployment benefits per unemployed divided by the compensation per employee.
7. Private non-agricultural sector.
Sources: Department of Labor, Bureau of Labor Statistics, Data Resources Incorporated, and OECD.

BASIC STATISTICS

BASIC STATISTICS:

INTERNATIONAL COMPARISONS

	Units	Reference period[1]	Australia	Austria	Belgium	C
Population						
Total	Thousands	1990	17 085	7 718	9 967	26
Inhabitants per sq. km	Number	1990	2	92	327	
Net average annual increase over previous 10 years ..	%	1990	1.5	0.2	0.1	
Employment						
Total civilian employment (TCE)[2]	Thousands	1990	7 850	3 412	3 726	12
Of which : Agriculture...................	% of TCE		5.6	7.9	2.7	
Industry	% of TCE		25.4	36.8	28.3	2
Services	% of TCE		69	55.3	69	7
Gross domestic product (GDP)						
At current prices and current exchange rates	Bill US $	1990	294.1	157.4	192.4	57
Per capita	US $		17 215 –	20 391	19 303	21
At current prices using current PPP's[3]	Bill US $	1990	271.7	127.4	163	51
Per capita	US $		15 900 ~	16 513	16 351	19
Average annual volume growth over previous 5 years .	%	1990	3.1	3.1	3.2	
Gross fixed capital formation (GFCF)	% of GDP	1990	22.9	24.3	20.3	2
Of which: *Machinery and equipment*	% of GDP		9.7	10.1	10.4	
Residential construction	% of GDP	1990	4.8	4.6	4.3	
Average annual volume growth over previous 5 years .	%	1990	2.4	4.6	9.5	
Gross saving ratio[4]	% of GDP	1990	19.7	26	21.8	1
General government						
Current expenditure on goods and services ...	% of GDP	1990	17.3	18	14.3	1
Current disbursements[5]	% of GDP	1990	34.9	44.9	53.1	
Current receipts	% of GDP	1990	35.1	46.7	49.5	4
Net official development assistance	Mill US $	1990	0.34	0.25	0.45	0
Indicators of living standards						
Private consumption per capita using current PPP's[3]	US $	1990	9 441	9 154	10 119	11
Passenger cars per 1 000 inhabitants	Number	1989	570	416	416	
Telephones per 1 000 inhabitants	Number	1989	550 (85)	540	500 (88)	
Television sets per 1 000 inhabitants	Number	1988	217	484 (89)	255	
Doctors per 1 000 inhabitants	Number	1990	2.3	2.1	3.4	
Infant mortality per 1 000 live births	Number	1990	8.2	7.8	7.9	
Wages and prices (average annual increase over previous 5 years)						
Wages (earnings or rates according to availability) ...	%	1990	5.6	5	3	
Consumer prices	%	1990	7.9	2.2	2.1	
Foreign trade						
Exports of goods, fob*	Mill US $	1990	39 813	40 985	118 291[7]	127
As % of GDP	%		13.5	26	61.5	2
Average annual increase over previous 5 years ...	%		11.9	19.1	17.1	
Imports of goods, cif*	Mill US $	1990	38 907	48 914	120 330[7]	116
As % of GDP	%		13.2	31.1	62.5	2
Average annual increase over previous 5 years ...	%		11	18.6	16.5	
Total official reserves[6]	Mill SDR's	1990	11 432	6 591	8 541[7]	12
As ratio of average monthly imports of goods	ratio		3.5	1.6	0.9	

* At current prices and exchange rates.
1. Unless otherwise stated.
2. According to the definitions used in OECD Labour Force Statistics.
3. PPP's = Purchasing Power Parities.
4. Gross saving = Gross national disposable income minus Private and Government consumption.
5. Current disbursements = Current expenditure on goods and services plus current transfers and payments of property income.
6. Gold included in reserves is valued at 35 SDR's per ounce. End of year.
7. Including Luxembourg.
8. Included in Belgium.

EMPLOYMENT OPPORTUNITIES

Economics Department, OECD

The Economics Department of the OECD offers challenging and rewarding opportunities to economists interested in applied policy analysis in an international environment. The Department's concerns extend across the entire field of economic policy analysis, both macro-economic and micro-economic. Its main task is to provide, for discussion by committees of senior officials from Member countries, documents and papers dealing with current policy concerns. Within this programme of work, three major responsibilities are:

- to prepare regular surveys of the economies of individual Member countries;
- to issue full twice-yearly reviews of the economic situation and prospects of the OECD countries in the context of world economic trends;
- to analyse specific policy issues in a medium-term context for theOECD as a whole, and to a lesser extent for the non-OECD countries.

The documents prepared for these purposes, together with much of the Department's other economic work, appear in published form in the *OECD Economic Outlook, OECD Economic Surveys, OECD Economic Studies* and the Department's *Working Papers* series.

The Department maintains a world econometric model, INTERLINK, which plays an important role in the preparation of the policy analyses and twice-yearly projections. The availability of extensive cross-country data bases and good computer resources facilitates comparative empirical analysis, much of which is incorporated into the model.

The Department is made up of about 75 professional economists from a variety of backgrounds and Member countries. Most projects are carried out by small teams and last from four to eighteen months. Within the Department, ideas and points of view are widely discussed; there is a lively professional interchange, and all professional staff have the opportunity to contribute actively to the programme of work.

Skills the Economics Department is looking for:

a) Solid competence in using the tools of both micro-economic and macro-economic theory to answer policy questions. Experience indicates that this normally requires the equivalent of a PH.D. in economics or substantial relevant professional experience to compensate for a lower degree.

b) Solid knowledge of economic statistics and quantitative methods; this includes how to identify data, estimate structural relationships, apply basic techniques of time series analysis, and test hypotheses. It is essential to be able to interpret results sensibly in an economic policy context.

c) A keen interest in and knowledge of policy issues, economic developments and their political/social contexts.

d) Interest and experience in analysing questions posed by policy-makers and presenting the results to them effectively and judiciously. Thus, work experience in government agencies or policy research institutions is an advantage.

e) The ability to write clearly, effectively, and to the point. The OECD is a bilingual organisation with French and English as the official languages. Candidates must have excellent knowledge of one of these languages, and some knowledge of the other. Knowledge of other languages might also be an advantage for certain posts.

f) For some posts, expertise in a particular area may be important, but a successful candidate is expected to be able to work on a broader range of topics relevant to the work of the Department. Thus, except in rare cases, the Department does not recruit narrow specialists.

g) The Department works on a tight time schedule and strict deadlines. Moreover, much of the work in the Department is carried out in small groups of economists. Thus, the ability to work with other economists from a variety of cultural and professional backgrounds, to supervise junior staff, and to produce work on time is important.

General Information

The salary for recruits depends on educational and professional background. Positions carry a basic salary from FF 262 512 or FF 323 916 for Administrators (economists) and from FF 375 708 for Principal Administrators (senior economists). This may be supplemented by expatriation and/or family allowances, depending on nationality, residence and family situation. Initial appointments are for a fixed term of two to three years.

Vacancies are open to candidates from OECD Member countries. The Organisation seeks to maintain an appropriate balance between female and male staff and among nationals from Member countries.

For further information on employment opportunities in the Economics Department, contact:

Administrative Unit
Economics Department
OECD
2, rue André-Pascal
75775 PARIS CEDEX 16
FRANCE

Applications citing "ECSUR", together with a detailed *curriculum vitae* in English or French, should be sent to the Head of Personnel at the above address.

MAIN SALES OUTLETS OF OECD PUBLICATIONS
PRINCIPAUX POINTS DE VENTE DES PUBLICATIONS DE L'OCDE

ARGENTINA – ARGENTINE
Carlos Hirsch S.R.L.
Galería Güemes, Florida 165, 4° Piso
1333 Buenos Aires   Tel. (1) 331.1787 y 331.2391
Telefax: (1) 331.1787

AUSTRALIA – AUSTRALIE
D.A. Book (Aust.) Pty. Ltd.
648 Whitehorse Road, P.O.B 163
Mitcham, Victoria 3132   Tel. (03) 873.4411
Telefax: (03) 873.5679

AUSTRIA – AUTRICHE
Gerold & Co.
Graben 31
Wien I   Tel. (0222) 533.50.14

BELGIUM – BELGIQUE
Jean De Lannoy
Avenue du Roi 202
B-1060 Bruxelles   Tel. (02) 538.51.69/538.08.41
Telefax: (02) 538.08.41

CANADA
Renouf Publishing Company Ltd.
1294 Algoma Road
Ottawa, ON K1B 3W8   Tel. (613) 741.4333
Telefax: (613) 741.5439
Stores:
61 Sparks Street
Ottawa, ON K1P 5R1   Tel. (613) 238.8985
211 Yonge Street
Toronto, ON M5B 1M4   Tel. (416) 363.3171
Les Éditions La Liberté Inc.
3020 Chemin Sainte-Foy
Sainte-Foy, PQ G1X 3V6   Tel. (418) 658.3763
Telefax: (418) 658.3763

Federal Publications
165 University Avenue
Toronto, ON M5H 3B8   Tel. (416) 581.1552
Telefax: (416) 581.1743

CHINA – CHINE
China National Publications Import
Export Corporation (CNPIEC)
16 Gongti E. Road, Chaoyang District
P.O. Box 88 or 50
Beijing 100704 PR   Tel. (01) 506.6688
Telefax: (01) 506.3101

DENMARK – DANEMARK
Munksgaard Export and Subscription Service
35, Nørre Søgade, P.O. Box 2148
DK-1016 København K   Tel. (33) 12.85.70
Telefax: (33) 12.93.87

FINLAND – FINLANDE
Akateeminen Kirjakauppa
Keskuskatu 1, P.O. Box 128
00100 Helsinki   Tel. (358 0) 12141
Telefax: (358 0) 121.4441

FRANCE
OECD/OCDE
Mail Orders/Commandes par correspondance:
2, rue André-Pascal
75775 Paris Cedex 16   Tel. (33-1) 45.24.82.00
Telefax: (33-1) 45.24.85.00 or (33-1) 45.24.81.76
Telex: 640048 OCDE

OECD Bookshop/Librairie de l'OCDE :
33, rue Octave-Feuillet
75016 Paris   Tel. (33-1) 45.24.81.67
(33-1) 45.24.81.81

Documentation Française
29, quai Voltaire
75007 Paris   Tel. 40.15.70.00

Gibert Jeune (Droit-Économie)
6, place Saint-Michel
75006 Paris   Tel. 43.25.91.19

Librairie du Commerce International
10, avenue d'Iéna
75016 Paris   Tel. 40.73.34.60
Librairie Dunod
Université Paris-Dauphine
Place du Maréchal de Lattre de Tassigny
75016 Paris   Tel. 47.27.18.56
Librairie Lavoisier
11, rue Lavoisier
75008 Paris   Tel. 42.65.39.95
Librairie L.G.D.J. - Montchrestien
20, rue Soufflot
75005 Paris   Tel. 46.33.89.85
Librairie des Sciences Politiques
30, rue Saint-Guillaume
75007 Paris   Tel. 45.48.36.02
P.U.F.
49, boulevard Saint-Michel
75005 Paris   Tel. 43.25.83.40
Librairie de l'Université
12a, rue Nazareth
13100 Aix-en-Provence   Tel. (16) 42.26.18.08
Documentation Française
165, rue Garibaldi
69003 Lyon   Tel. (16) 78.63.32.23
Librairie Decitre
29, place Bellecour
69002 Lyon   Tel. (16) 72.40.54.54

GERMANY – ALLEMAGNE
OECD Publications and Information Centre
Schedestrasse 7
D-W 5300 Bonn 1   Tel. (0228) 21.60.45
Telefax: (0228) 26.11.04

GREECE – GRÈCE
Librairie Kauffmann
Mavrokordatou 9
106 78 Athens   Tel. 322.21.60
Telefax: 363.39.67

HONG-KONG
Swindon Book Co. Ltd.
13–15 Lock Road
Kowloon, Hong Kong   Tel. 366.80.31
Telefax: 739.49.75

ICELAND – ISLANDE
Mál Mog Menning
Laugavegi 18, Pósthólf 392
121 Reykjavik   Tel. 162.35.23

INDIA – INDE
Oxford Book and Stationery Co.
Scindia House
New Delhi 110001   Tel.(11) 331.5896/5308
Telefax: (11) 332.5993
17 Park Street
Calcutta 700016   Tel. 240832

INDONESIA – INDONÉSIE
Pdii-Lipi
P.O. Box 269/JKSMG/88
Jakarta 12790   Tel. 583467
Telex: 62 875

IRELAND – IRLANDE
TDC Publishers – Library Suppliers
12 North Frederick Street
Dublin 1   Tel. 74.48.35/74.96.77
Telefax: 74.84.16

ISRAEL
Electronic Publications only
Publications électroniques seulement
Sophist Systems Ltd.
71 Allenby Street
Tel-Aviv 65134   Tel. 3-29.00.21
Telefax: 3-29.92.39

ITALY – ITALIE
Libreria Commissionaria Sansoni
Via Duca di Calabria 1/1
50125 Firenze   Tel. (055) 64.54.15
Telefax: (055) 64.12.57

Via Bartolini 29
20155 Milano   Tel. (02) 36.50.83

Editrice e Libreria Herder
Piazza Montecitorio 120
00186 Roma   Tel. 679.46.28
Telefax: 678.47.51

Libreria Hoepli
Via Hoepli 5
20121 Milano   Tel. (02) 86.54.46
Telefax: (02) 805.28.86

Libreria Scientifica
Dott. Lucio de Biasio 'Aeiou'
Via Coronelli, 6
20146 Milano   Tel. (02) 48.95.45.52
Telefax: (02) 48.95.45.48

JAPAN – JAPON
OECD Publications and Information Centre
Landic Akasaka Building
2-3-4 Akasaka, Minato-ku
Tokyo 107   Tel. (81.3) 3586.2016
Telefax: (81.3) 3584.7929

KOREA – CORÉE
Kyobo Book Centre Co. Ltd.
P.O. Box 1658, Kwang Hwa Moon
Seoul   Tel. 730.78.91
Telefax: 735.00.30

MALAYSIA – MALAISIE
Co-operative Bookshop Ltd.
University of Malaya
P.O. Box 1127, Jalan Pantai Baru
59700 Kuala Lumpur
Malaysia   Tel. 756.5000/756.5425
Telefax: 757.3661

NETHERLANDS – PAYS-BAS
SDU Uitgeverij
Christoffel Plantijnstraat 2
Postbus 20014
2500 EA's-Gravenhage   Tel. (070 3) 78.99.11
Voor bestellingen: Tel. (070 3) 78.98.80
Telefax: (070 3) 47.63.51

NEW ZEALAND
NOUVELLE-ZÉLANDE
Legislation Services
P.O. Box 12418
Thorndon, Wellington   Tel. (04) 496.5652
Telefax: (04) 496.5698

NORWAY – NORVÈGE
Narvesen Info Center – NIC
Bertrand Narvesens vei 2
P.O. Box 6125 Etterstad
0602 Oslo 6   Tel. (02) 57.33.00
Telefax: (02) 68.19.01

PAKISTAN
Mirza Book Agency
65 Shahrah Quaid-E-Azam
Lahore 3   Tel. 66.839
Telex: 44886 UBL PK. Attn: MIRZA BK

PORTUGAL
Livraria Portugal
Rua do Carmo 70-74
Apart. 2681
1117 Lisboa Codex   Tel.: (01) 347.49.82/3/4/5
Telefax: (01) 347.02.64

SINGAPORE – SINGAPOUR
Information Publications Pte. Ltd.
41, Kallang Pudding, No. 04-03
Singapore 1334   Tel. 741.5166
                         Telefax: 742.9356

SPAIN – ESPAGNE
Mundi-Prensa Libros S.A.
Castelló 37, Apartado 1223
Madrid 28001   Tel. (91) 431.33.99
                         Telefax: (91) 575.39.98
Libreria Internacional AEDOS
Consejo de Ciento 391
08009 – Barcelona   Tel. (93) 488.34.92
                         Telefax: (93) 487.76.59
Llibreria de la Generalitat
Palau Moja
Rambla dels Estudis, 118
08002 – Barcelona
       (Subscripcions) Tel. (93) 318.80.12
       (Publicacions) Tel. (93) 302.67.23
                         Telefax: (93) 412.18.54

SRI LANKA
Centre for Policy Research
c/o Colombo Agencies Ltd.
No. 300-304, Galle Road
Colombo 3   Tel. (1) 574240, 573551-2
                      Telefax: (1) 575394, 510711

SWEDEN – SUÈDE
Fritzes Fackboksföretaget
Box 16356
Regeringsgatan 12
103 27 Stockholm   Tel. (08) 23.89.00
                         Telefax: (08) 20.50.21
Subscription Agency-Agence d'abonnements
Wennergren-Williams AB
Nordenflychtsvägen 74
Box 30004
104 25 Stockholm   Tel. (08) 13.67.00
                         Telefax: (08) 618.62.36

SWITZERLAND – SUISSE
Maditec S.A. (Books and Periodicals - Livres
et périodiques)
Chemin des Palettes 4
1020 Renens/Lausanne   Tel. (021) 635.08.65
                         Telefax: (021) 635.07.80

Librairie Payot
Service des Publications Internationales
Case postale 3212
1002 Lausanne   Tel. (021) 341.33.48
                         Telefax: (021) 341.33.45

Librairie Unilivres
6, rue de Candolle
1205 Genève   Tel. (022) 320.26.23
                         Telefax: (022) 329.73.18

Subscription Agency - Agence d'abonnement
Naville S.A.
38 avenue Vibert
1227 Carouge   Tél.: (022) 308.05.56/57
                         Telefax: (022) 308.05.88

See also – Voir aussi :
OECD Publications and Information Centre
Schedestrasse 7
D-W 5300 Bonn 1 (Germany)
                         Tel. (49.228) 21.60.45
                         Telefax: (49.228) 26.11.04

TAIWAN – FORMOSE
Good Faith Worldwide Int'l. Co. Ltd.
9th Floor, No. 118, Sec. 2
Chung Hsiao E. Road
Taipei   Tel. (02) 391.7396/391.7397
                         Telefax: (02) 394.9176

THAILAND – THAÏLANDE
Suksit Siam Co. Ltd.
113, 115 Fuang Nakhon Rd.
Opp. Wat Rajbopith
Bangkok 10200   Tel. (662) 251.1630
                         Telefax: (662) 236.7783

TURKEY – TURQUIE
Kültur Yayinlari Is-Türk Ltd. Sti.
Atatürk Bulvari No. 191/Kat. 13
Kavaklidere/Ankara   Tel. 428.11.40 Ext. 2458
Dolmabahce Cad. No. 29
Besiktas/Istanbul   Tel. 160.71.88
                         Telex: 43482B

UNITED KINGDOM – ROYAUME-UNI
HMSO
Gen. enquiries   Tel. (071) 873 0011
Postal orders only:
P.O. Box 276, London SW8 5DT
Personal Callers HMSO Bookshop
49 High Holborn, London WC1V 6HB
                         Telefax: (071) 873 8200
Branches at: Belfast, Birmingham, Bristol, Edin-
burgh, Manchester

UNITED STATES – ÉTATS-UNIS
OECD Publications and Information Centre
2001 L Street N.W., Suite 700
Washington, D.C. 20036-4910 Tel. (202) 785.6323
                         Telefax: (202) 785.0350

VENEZUELA
Libreria del Este
Avda F. Miranda 52, Aptdo. 60337
Edificio Galipán
Caracas 106   Tel. 951.1705/951.2307/951.1297
                      Telegram: Libreste Caracas

Subscription to OECD periodicals may also be
placed through main subscription agencies.

Les abonnements aux publications périodiques de
l'OCDE peuvent être souscrits auprès des
principales agences d'abonnement.

Orders and inquiries from countries where Distribu-
tors have not yet been appointed should be sent to:
OECD Publications Service, 2 rue André-Pascal,
75775 Paris Cedex 16, France.

Les commandes provenant de pays où l'OCDE n'a
pas encore désigné de distributeur devraient être
adressées à : OCDE, Service des Publications,
2, rue André-Pascal, 75775 Paris Cedex 16, France.

10-1992

PRINTED IN FRANCE

•

OECD PUBLICATIONS
2 rue André-Pascal
75775 PARIS CEDEX 16
No. 46341
(10 92 02 1) ISBN 92-64-13775-0
ISSN 0376-6438

•